INTRODUCING
ISSUES
WITH

OPPOSING VIEWPOINTS®

GAY
MARRIAGE

Other books in the Introducing Issues
with Opposing Viewpoints series:

AIDS
Alcohol
Civil Liberties
Cloning
The Death Penalty
Gangs
Genetic Engineering
Smoking
Terrorism

INTRODUCING ISSUES WITH

OPPOSING VIEWPOINTS®

GAY MARRIAGE

Lauri S. Friedman, *Book Editor*

Bruce Glassman, *Vice President*
Bonnie Szumski, *Publisher, Series Editor*
Helen Cothran, *Managing Editor*

OPPOSING
VIEWPOINTS®
SERIES

GREENHAVEN PRESS
An imprint of Thomson Gale, a part of The Thomson Corporation

THOMSON
—★—™
GALE

Detroit • New York • San Francisco • San Diego • New Haven, Conn. • Waterville, Maine • London • Munich

THOMSON

━━━★━━━ ™

GALE

© 2006 Thomson Gale, a part of The Thomson Corporation.

Thomson and Star Logo are trademarks and Gale and Greenhaven Press are registered trademarks used herein under license.

For more information, contact
Greenhaven Press
27500 Drake Rd.
Farmington Hills, MI 48331-3535
Or you can visit our Internet site at http://www.gale.com

LIBRARY OF CONGRESS CATALOGING-IN-PUBLICATION DATA
Gay marriage / Lauri S. Friedman, book editor.
p. cm. — (Introducing issues with opposing viewpoints)
Includes bibliographical references and index.
ISBN 0-7377-3222-9 (lib. bdg. : alk. paper)
1. Same-sex marriage—United States. 2. Same-sex marriage. I. Friedman, Lauri S.
II. Series.
HQ1034.U5G39 2006
306.84'8'0973—dc22
2005045988

Printed in the United States of America

CONTENTS

Indulging in a wide spectrum of ideas, beliefs, and perspectives is a critical cornerstone of democracy. After all, it is often debates over differences of opinion, such as whether to legalize abortion, how to treat prisoners, or when to enact the death penalty that shape our society and drive it forward. Such diversity of thought is frequently regarded as the hallmark of a healthy and civilized culture. As the Reverend Clifford Schutjer of the First Congregational Church in Mansfield, Ohio, declared in a 2001 sermon, "Surrounding oneself with only like-minded people, restricting what we listen to or read only to what we find agreeable is irresponsible. Refusing to entertain doubts once we make up our minds is a subtle but deadly form of arrogance." With this advice in mind, Introducing Issues with Opposing Viewpoints books aim to open readers' minds to the critically divergent views that comprise our world's most important debates.

Introducing Issues with Opposing Viewpoints simplifies for students the enormous and often overwhelming mass of material now available via print and electronic media. Collected in every volume is an array of opinions that capture the essence of a particular controversy or topic. Introducing Issues with Opposing Viewpoints books embody the spirit of nineteenth-century journalist Charles A. Dana's axiom: "Fight for your opinions, but do not believe that they contain the whole truth, or the only truth." Absorbing such contrasting opinions teaches students to analyze the strength of an argument and compare it to its opposition. From this process readers can inform and strengthen their own opinions, or be exposed to new information that will change their minds. Introducing Issues with Opposing Viewpoints is a mosaic of different voices. The authors are statesmen, pundits, academics, journalists, corporations, and ordinary people who have felt compelled to share their experiences and ideas in a public forum. Their words have been collected from newspapers, journals, books, speeches, interviews, and the Internet, the fastest growing body of opinionated material in the world.

Introducing Issues with Opposing Viewpoints shares many of the well-known features of its critically acclaimed parent series, Opposing Viewpoints. The articles are presented in a pro/con format, allowing readers to absorb divergent perspectives side by side. Active reading questions preface each viewpoint, requiring the student to approach the material thoughtfully and carefully. Useful charts, graphs, and cartoons supplement each article. A thorough introduction provides readers with crucial background on an issue. An annotated bibliography points the reader toward articles, books, and Web sites that contain additional information on the topic. An appendix of organizations to contact contains a wide variety of charities, nonprofit organizations, political groups, and private enterprises that each hold a position on the issue at hand. Finally, a comprehensive index allows readers to locate content quickly and efficiently.

Introducing Issues with Opposing Viewpoints is also significantly different from Opposing Viewpoints. As the series title implies, its presentation will help introduce students to the concept of opposing viewpoints, and learn to use this material to aid in critical writing and debate. The series' four-color, accessible format makes the books attractive and inviting to readers of all levels. In addition, each viewpoint has been carefully edited to maximize a reader's understanding of the content. Short but thorough viewpoints capture the essence of an argument. A substantial, thought-provoking essay question placed at the end of each viewpoint asks the student to further investigate the issues raised in the viewpoint, compare and contrast two authors' arguments, or consider how one might go about forming an opinion on the topic at hand. Each viewpoint contains sidebars that include at-a-glance information and handy statistics. A Facts About section located in the back of the book further supplies students with relevant facts and figures.

Following in the tradition of the Opposing Viewpoints series, Greenhaven Press continues to provide readers with invaluable exposure to the controversial issues that shape our world. As John Stuart Mill once wrote: "The only way in which a human being can make some approach to knowing the whole of a subject is by hearing what can be said about it by persons of every variety of opinion and studying all modes in which it can be looked at by every character of mind. No wise man ever acquired his wisdom in any mode but this." It is to this principle that Introducing Issues with Opposing Viewpoints books are dedicated.

"What is marriage for? Why have laws about it? Why care whether people get married or stay married? . . . These are the questions that same-sex marriage raises. Our answers will affect not only gay and lesbian families, but marriage as a whole."

—Maggie Gallagher, columnist for the *Weekly Standard*

Although the issue of gay marriage has been a fairly heated topic of discussion for many years, the issue was catapulted into the public spotlight in 2003 and 2004, when the state of Massachusetts legalized gay marriage, and the cities of San Francisco, California, New Paltz, New York, and Sandoval County, New Mexico, briefly handed out marriage licenses to same-sex couples. In response to these actions, President George W. Bush proposed amending the U.S. Constitution to ban gay marriage by stating that marriage should be legal only between a man and a woman. Together, these events touched off a fierce and polarizing debate about marriage that sparks an emotional defense of values and identity from all who hold opinions on the topic. At the heart of the controversy over gay marriage are vastly different understandings of a seemingly simple question: What is the purpose of marriage?

To some people, the purpose of marriage should be solely to make and raise children. Many religious understandings of marriage stress that sexual contact between men and women should result in children. Because people of the same sex cannot produce children, opponents argue gay marriage does not benefit society and thus should not be encouraged. However, same-sex couples reject the idea that having children is a universal or integral part of marriage. They point out that heterosexual couples who are sterile, or who simply choose not to have children, are no more barred from marriage than any other heterosexual couple. Thus, childlessness should not exclude gay couples from marriage.

To others, marriage is the way two people show their love and commitment to each other, and many gay couples say that this is why they want the institution of marriage extended to them. As author E.J.

A gay couple is showered with flower petals after filing for a marriage license in a Boston courthouse. Same-sex marriages were legalized in Massachusetts in 2004.

Graff says, when most people say "'I am getting married,' they don't mean, 'I'm hustling over to some public functionary to get a government license.' They mean, 'I am going to stand up in front of my . . . community and openly declare my commitment to love and care for this person.'" Yet opponents of gay marriage charge that it is unfair to alter the institution of marriage so that gay couples can prove they are in love and committed. They say that the word marriage inherently connotes a union between one man and one woman, and any attempt to divorce it from this meaning dissolves the essence of marriage entirely. As author Orson Scott Card has remarked, "Giving 'legal sanction' to homosexuals marrying and calling their contract a 'marriage' does not make it a marriage. It simply removes *marriage* as a legitimate word for the real thing."

Yet another meaning of marriage is found in the many financial and legal opportunities that are bestowed upon married couples by the government. There are an estimated 1,138 federal rights and up to 300 state-level rights that accompany a marriage license. These include hospital visitation rights, survivor benefits, inheritance rights, tax rights, and many other significant benefits. Supporters of gay marriage believe that same-sex couples should be allowed these rights; indeed, some argue that denying committed gay couples the legal and financial benefits of marriage is akin to relegating them to second-class citizens. "The fight for queer civil rights is as important to the 21st century as the fight for black civil rights was to the 20th," argues author Victoria A. Brownworth. On the other hand, opponents of

Some people believe that the sole purpose of marriage is to produce and raise children. By this definition, same-sex couples should be barred from marriage.

gay marriage believe that same-sex relationships can never count as a true marriage, and thus argue that extending them the rights and privileges of marriage is inappropriate.

A third viewpoint exists, however, and is gaining ground as a feasible solution to the debate over same-sex marriage: civil unions. Civil unions are arrangements that provide gay couples with rights and benefits that are similar to those that married people have. However, civil unions are not quite marriages—they are simply legal arrangements, lacking the sacred or traditional quality of a marriage. Many liberal and conservative Americans believe this compromise would settle the marriage debate: Rights and privileges would be granted to same-sex couples, but marriage and its religious and moral implications would remain an institution solely for heterosexual couples. In fact, according to a Quinnipiac University poll taken in December 2004, 45 percent of

In 2004 protesters outside the Massachusetts State House demonstrate against the legislature's move to ban gay marriage in favor of civil unions for homosexual couples.

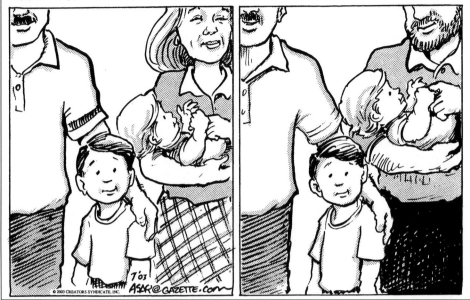

NEWS ITEM: REP. MARILYN MUSGRAVE, R-COLO., SPONSORS A CONSTITUTIONAL AMENDMENT WHICH DEFINES MARRIAGE AS BETWEEN A MAN AND A WOMAN!
WHICH INSTITUTION DO **YOU** THINK IS BEST EQUIPPED TO RAISE CHILDREN?

Source: Asay. © 2003 by Creators Syndicate. Reproduced by permission.

Americans surveyed said they would support civil unions. Only 31 percent, in contrast, said they would support gay marriage. Already, several states extend some type of civil union or domestic partnership rights to same-sex couples, while the state of Vermont has entirely legalized civil unions for same-sex couples, granting them all of the rights that married couples have. As author Andrew Koppelman claims, "Civil unions are the most politically stable answer for the next decade or so. Given the depth of our moral disagreement, that is saying a lot."

Many people, however, do not approve of civil unions, or of offering any rights to gay couples. Therefore, Americans continue to debate the definition of marriage and who should benefit from it. The viewpoints presented in *Introducing Issues with Opposing Viewpoints: Gay Marriage* offer further insight into the key debates surrounding this current and controversial topic.

CHAPTER 1

Should Homosexuals Be Allowed to Marry?

During a demonstration against legalized gay marriage in Massachusetts, this man's sign expresses the belief of many Americans on the issue.

VIEWPOINT 1

A Constitutional Amendment Should Ban Gay Marriage

George W. Bush

"I call upon the Congress to promptly pass, and send to the states for ratification, an amendment to our Constitution defining and protecting marriage."

In the following viewpoint, President George W. Bush argues that the United States must adopt a constitutional amendment that defines marriage as a union between heterosexuals. The amendment would ban gay marriage in all fifty states. Bush charges that the actions of a few isolated judges and other authorities have threatened democracy by imposing gay marriage on the public without the public's approval. Furthermore, because these judges have tampered with the laws in scattered cities and states across the nation, they have created a state of confusion over what marriage is and who is entitled to it. Therefore, the United States should amend the Constitution by clarifying that marriage can only be legal between a man and a woman and no other combination of people. The president concludes that such an amendment will protect marriage's place as an enduring human institution that safeguards children and stabilizes society.

George W. Bush is the forty-third president of the United States.

George W. Bush, "President Calls for a Constitutional Amendment Protecting Marriage," www.whitehouse.gov, February 24, 2004.

AS YOU READ, CONSIDER THE FOLLOWING QUESTIONS:
1. What was the content of the 1998 Defense of Marriage Act?
2. What does the president mean when he uses the word *activist* to refer to certain courts and judges?
3. According to President Bush, what events took place in San Francisco, and why were they unlawful?

THE PRESIDENT: Good morning. [In 1998], Congress passed, and [former] President [Bill] Clinton signed, the Defense of Marriage Act, which defined marriage for purposes of federal law as the legal union between one man and one woman as husband and wife.

The Act passed the House of Representatives by a vote of 342 to 67, and the Senate by a vote of 85 to 14. Those congressional votes and the passage of similar defensive marriage laws in 38 states express an overwhelming consensus in our country for protecting the institution of marriage.

> **FAST FACT**
>
> In the 2004 general elections, voters in eleven states elected to adopt amendments that ban gay marriage in their state constitution.

Violations of Democracy

In recent months, however, some activist judges and local officials have made an aggressive attempt to redefine marriage. In Massachusetts, four judges on the highest court have indicated they will order the issuance of marriage licenses to applicants of the same gender in May of [2004]. In San Francisco, city officials have issued thousands of marriage licenses to people of the same gender, contrary to the California family code. That code, which clearly defines marriage as the union of a man and a woman, was approved overwhelmingly by the voters of California. A county in New Mexico has also issued marriage licenses to applicants of the same gender. And unless action is taken, we can expect more arbitrary court decisions, more litigation, more defiance of the law by local officials, all of which adds to uncertainty.

After more than two centuries of American jurisprudence, and millennia of human experience, a few judges and local authorities are presuming to change the most fundamental institution of civilization. Their actions have created confusion on an issue that requires clarity.

On a matter of such importance, the voice of the people must be heard. Activist courts have left the people with one recourse. If we are to prevent the meaning of marriage from being changed forever, our nation must enact a constitutional amendment to protect marriage in America. Decisive and democratic action is needed, because attempts to redefine marriage in a single state or city could have serious consequences throughout the country.

Marriage Must Be Protected Under the Constitution

The Constitution says that full faith and credit shall be given in each state to the public acts and records and judicial proceedings of every other state. Those who want to change the meaning of marriage will claim that this provision requires all states and cities to recognize same-sex marriages performed anywhere in America. Congress attempted

Many gay couples, like this one in San Francisco, flocked to courthouses after officials in some cities legalized gay marriage in 2004. The marriages, however, were later invalidated.

to address this problem in the Defense of Marriage Act, by declaring that no state must accept another state's definition of marriage. My administration will vigorously defend this act of Congress.

Yet there is no assurance that the Defense of Marriage Act will not, itself, be struck down by activist courts. In that event, every state would be forced to recognize any relationship that judges in Boston or officials in San Francisco choose to call a marriage. Furthermore,

A minister in Boston signs a wedding certificate for a gay couple. The Defense of Marriage Act stipulates that individual states can reject the validity of gay marriages sanctioned by other states.

In 2004 President George W. Bush announces that he intends to support a constitutional ban on gay marriage.

even if the Defense of Marriage Act is upheld, the law does not protect marriage within any state or city.

For all these reasons, the defense of marriage requires a constitutional amendment. An amendment to the Constitution is never to be undertaken lightly. The amendment process has addressed many serious matters of national concern. And the preservation of marriage

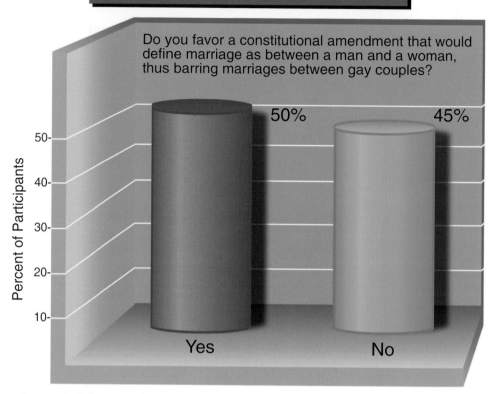

Gay Marriage in the United States

Do you favor a constitutional amendment that would define marriage as between a man and a woman, thus barring marriages between gay couples?

50%

45%

Percent of Participants

50-
40-
30-
20-
10-

Yes

No

Source: *USA Today*/CNN Gallup Poll, May 5–7, July 25–26, 2003.

rises to this level of national importance. The union of a man and woman is the most enduring human institution—honored and encouraged in all cultures and by every religious faith. Ages of experience have taught humanity that the commitment of a husband and wife to love and to serve one another promotes the welfare of children and the stability of society.

The Interests of All

Marriage cannot be severed from its cultural, religious and natural roots without weakening the good influence of society. Government, by recognizing and protecting marriage, serves the interests of all. Today I call upon the Congress to promptly pass, and send to the states for ratification, an amendment to our Constitution defining and protecting marriage as a union of man and woman as husband and wife. The amendment should fully protect marriage, while leaving the state legislatures free to make their own choices in defining legal arrangements other than marriage.

America is a free society, which limits the role of government in the lives of our citizens. This commitment of freedom, however, does not require the redefinition of one of our most basic social institutions. Our government should respect every person, and protect the institution of marriage. There is no contradiction between these responsibilities. We should also conduct this difficult debate in a manner worthy of our country, without bitterness or anger.

In all that lies ahead, let us match strong convictions with kindness and goodwill and decency.

EVALUATING THE AUTHORS' ARGUMENTS:

In the viewpoint you just read, President Bush argues in favor of a constitutional amendment to ban gay marriage. In the following viewpoint, author Joe Capello argues against such an amendment. After reading both viewpoints, what is your opinion on the necessity of a constitutional amendment to ban gay marriage? What benefits or drawbacks do you think such an amendment would have? Explain your reasoning, and use evidence from the viewpoints to support your answer.

A Constitutional Amendment Should Not Ban Gay Marriage

Joe Capello

"Amending the Constitution in an attempt to permanently enshrine bigotry and discrimination is . . . immoral."

In the following viewpoint, author Joe Capello argues that the United States should not adopt an amendment banning gay marriage because the Constitution has traditionally been used to protect minority groups, not discriminate against them. The author compares the fight for gay marriage to that of interracial couples who were barred from marrying until the 1960s. Capello contends that America must realize that allowing a gay couple to marry will not destroy the institution of marriage. In fact, he suggests that legalizing gay marriage will strengthen the institution of marriage by inviting more people to engage in unions of trust and commitment and by extending important rights to children. The author concludes by saying the attempt to block gay marriage represents the final battle of conservative America to paint homosexuals as immoral perverts. He implores Americans to see gay partners as they would any loving, committed couple.

Joe Capello is a gay resident of Denver, Colorado. He has been a guest writer for the *Denver Post*.

AS YOU READ, CONSIDER THE FOLLOWING QUESTIONS:
1. What point is the author making when he mentions that gay marriage is legal in Canada?
2. According to the author, how can children benefit from gay marriage?
3. Why does the author characterize the proposal to adopt a constitutional amendment banning gay marriage as "mean-spirited"?

My hopes of legally marrying the man I've loved for nearly a decade were crushed when President [George W.] Bush called for a constitutional amendment to ban gay marriage. He said that the amendment has overwhelming support from the American people and that, "on a matter of such importance, the voice of the people must be heard."

The Constitution Should Protect, Not Discriminate

I respectfully disagree. The U.S. Constitution was forged to protect minorities like us from the whims and fears of the (heterosexual) majority when it comes to fundamental rights like marriage. The Constitution stood as protection for those interracial couples who wanted to legally wed in the 1960s, and it's going to protect us now. That's why the politicians are preaching that the Constitution must be changed.

U.S. Rep. Marilyn Musgrave calls the threat of my marriage "a real and present danger that will undermine the foundation" of American society. The president's spokesman says that time is of the essence and "we need to act now." Listening to the politicians, you'd think we're

> **FAST FACT**
>
> Amendments to the Constitution typically expand the rights of Americans. The only other time that the Constitution was amended to specifically ban something was in 1920, when for thirteen years alcohol was federally prohibited.

threatened with the end of civilization as we know it. Never mind that gay marriage is already legal in Canada.

Enough already with the hysterical rhetoric. I realize they're merely politicking, but there's something hateful about people seeking a political gain at my personal expense. But they're going to lose this battle, because the arguments against my right to marry my mate simply don't hold water.

Representative Marilyn Musgrave (center) and Senator Wayne Allard of Colorado urge Congress to act against the "danger" of allowing gays to marry.

One of the reasons gay couples seek the right to marry is to publicly demonstrate their love and commitment to one another.

Arguments Against Gay Marriage Are Weak

For starters, my desire to legally marry is not an attack on the institution of marriage or—as Musgrave describes it on her website—"a crisis far more severe than any current danger marriage is facing." Marriage is a mess, certainly, but blame that on infidelity, domestic violence and a ridiculous divorce rate, not on gay nesters. It's not about the "sanctity" of marriage, either. With the advent of reality TV, that argument went out the window faster than you can say "Who Wants to Marry a Millionaire?"

It's not about religion. No church will be required to perform a homosexual wedding ceremony. This is about city hall and equal benefits. It's about rights, not rites. Why not a civil union? I'm not a second-class

citizen. This country already tried "separate but equal" classes of citizenship, but the Supreme Court put an end to that legal fiction in the 1950s [when it outlawed segregation].

It's not about morality. Being gay and married is perfectly moral. Most Americans may disagree today, but even they must admit that society's sense of right and wrong changes over time. It was considered perfectly moral to deny marriage licenses to interracial couples for the nearly first 200 years of our nation's history. Nowadays, such denial is considered immoral. Amending the Constitution in an attempt to permanently enshrine bigotry and discrimination is likewise immoral.

It's not about "protecting the children." The children of today's married couples do need protection from domestic abuse and the trauma of divorce, but banning gay marriages won't bring them any relief. Besides, aren't the children of gay couples equally deserving of legal protections? Those who are fortunate enough to be adopted by a committed gay couple deserve the protections afforded only to parents who are legally married, like inheritance rights, child support and Social Security survivor benefits.

Homosexuals Are Human Beings Who Deserve Rights

Finally, it's not about sex. As any couple who's been together for years will attest, it's about love, commitment, mutual respect and support. And there's the rub! Now you can understand why opponents of gay marriage are so hysterical. If gay people are allowed to legally marry in this country, the American public eventually will come to view us as human beings deserving of equal civil rights who—for reasons we ourselves can't articulate—have paired up with a partner of the same sex. It will signify final defeat for our opponents, who for years have painted us as just sex-crazed perverts.

I refuse to believe that this mean-spirited amendment will garner the support of the 38 state legislatures that need to ratify it. In the end, it may not matter because in my heart, where God lives, I'm already married.

EVALUATING THE AUTHOR'S ARGUMENTS:

In the viewpoint you just read, the author mentions that for much of America's history, interracial marriages were considered immoral, but society's opinion of them changed with time. Considering what you know about the gay marriage debate, do you think attitudes about same-sex marriage will change with time? Why or why not? Explain your answer.

Homosexual Couples Should Seek Civil Unions

Andrew Koppelman

"Civil unions are the most politically stable answer for the next decade or so."

In the following viewpoint, author Andrew Koppelman argues that a good compromise to the controversy over gay marriage would be to unite same-sex couples by civil union, which gives them nearly all of the benefits of marriage but stops short of calling the arrangement "marriage." The author points out that there is a surprisingly high level of public support for same-sex relationships when they are labeled "domestic partnerships" or "civil unions." The label "marriage," on the other hand, invokes religious concepts that are not typically applied to same-sex relationships and is thus passionately denounced by opponents. Meanwhile, although gay couples seek to enter the institution of wedlock in the same way as heterosexual couples, they can achieve the most important benefits of marriage through the civil union arrangement. To avoid the problem, therefore, the author suggests that both sides settle on civil unions as a compromise

Andrew Koppelman, "Civil Conflict and Same-Sex Civil Unions," *The Responsive Community,* Spring/Summer 2004. Copyright © 2004 by Andrew Koppelman. Reproduced by permission.

to the fierce debate over marriage. Although civil unions are not the ideal solution for either party, the author concludes they are the best arrangement for the immediate future.

Andrew Koppelman is a professor of law and political science at Northwestern University. He has written extensively in defense of same-sex marriage and gay rights.

AS YOU READ, CONSIDER THE FOLLOWING QUESTIONS:
1. According to the author, why are religious conservatives hesitant to establish civil unions for same-sex couples?
2. What is one complaint the gay community has about civil unions?
3. What do you think the author means when he describes civil unions as "the safest territory to occupy"?

The controversy over same-sex marriage is a battle between two competing moral visions. Each entails a single, unified national solution to the marriage question, which has no room for the other. Neither vision is likely to prevail in the near future. We have already begun a period of stalemate that is likely to persist for some time. . . .

Unsurprisingly both sides are pushing for total victory. Gay rights advocates (myself among them) have long argued that the denial of marriage rights to same-sex couples violates the U.S. Constitution, both because discrimination against gays is as invidious as racial discrimination and because the heterosexuality requirement discriminates on the basis of gender: men, but not women, can marry women. Were courts to accept this argument, same-sex marriages would have to be recognized throughout the United States. President [George W.] Bush has responded, at the insistence of his allies on the religious right [that is, conservatives], by proposing an equally uniform solution: a constitutional amendment that would *ban* same-sex marriage anywhere in the United States.

A compromise position has emerged: "civil unions," which have all the benefits of marriage without the name. The idea was originated by the Vermont Supreme Court, which in 1999 responded to a lawsuit

In 2004 Massachusetts senator Stan Rosenberg (left) announces to a crowd of protesters that state legislators have just voted to ban gay marriage in favor of civil unions.

by ordering the legislature to provide same-sex couples with the benefits of marriage, but not necessarily the name. The legislature complied and [former] Governor Howard Dean signed the bill, which remains the law in Vermont. A similar measure, in the form of a proposed amendment to the state constitution, has been offered as the moderate compromise response to the Massachusetts Supreme Court's recent decision mandating same-sex marriage in that state.

Support for "Civil Unions," Disdain for "Marriage"

This position has considerable political attractions. Americans oppose same-sex marriage by overwhelming margins, typically two to one against. But polls also show that the label of "marriage" is all that many really care about. So long as that line isn't crossed, they are quite willing to let the law recognize same-sex relationships. One recent poll found that health insurance for gay partners was supported by 58 percent of Americans, and 54 percent thought (contrary to the federal Defense of Marriage Act) that partners should get Social Security benefits. (Only 34 percent of those polled thought there should be legally sanctioned same-sex marriages.) When people are asked about giving gay couples *all* the same legal rights as married couples, another poll found, the split is a third in favor, a third against, and a third who don't care.

On the other hand, if the word "marriage" is used, not only do the numbers shift, but passions suddenly run very high. Richard Viguerie, the most experienced conservative direct-mail fundraiser in the country, told the *New York Times* after the Massachusetts decision legalizing same-sex marriage in that state that same-sex marriage will be a

An elderly couple prays that the California state assembly will vote to ban gay marriage. Members of the religious right are also opposed to civil unions for gay couples.

better fundraising issue than abortion. "I have never seen anything that has energized and provoked our grass roots like this issue, including *Roe v. Wade* [the controversial case that legalized abortion]," said Richard Land, president of the Ethics and Religious Liberty Commission of the Southern Baptist Convention, which has 16 million members. . . .

So why not just compromise and enact an equivalent without the label? In Vermont, and shortly in California as a result of recent legislation, "civil unions" and "domestic partnerships" give same-sex couples nearly all the legal benefits of marriage. When California enacted its law, with no prodding from any court, the national press hardly even picked up the story.

Both Sides Wary of Compromise

There are two reasons why gay rights advocates resist the "civil unions" compromise. First, they also buy into the sanctification narrative, and they want their relationships sanctified, too. [Gay rights activist]

Pro- and con- demonstrators face off at a 2004 rally. While many Americans favor extending full civil rights to gay couples, they reject the term "marriage" to describe their union.

Jonathan Rauch thus writes that "marriage is society's most fundamental institution. To bar any class of people from marrying as they
choose is an extraordinary deprivation." [Author] Andrew Sullivan
describes marriage as "the social institution that defines for many people the most meaningful part of their lives." More is at issue here than
legal benefits.

The second objection to civil unions is that gays don't want second
class status, and that's what civil unions amount to. The Massachusetts
Supreme Court rejected such unions,
because they "would have the effect of
maintaining and fostering a stigma of
exclusion that the Constitution pro-
hibits." Here gays can draw on an
American redemption narrative: the
long struggle for equality. The gay
struggle for equality in many ways
resembles the struggle against racism.
Both narratives prominently feature
vicious, irrational prejudice, gang violence met with official indifference,
pervasive discrimination, and an unre-
sponsive political system. Separate but
equal has an unattractive history.

Civil unions are no more popular
with the religious right. Such unions give state recognition to same-
sex relationships as such, implying that such relationships are in some
way legitimate. Once those relationships are thus legitimated, religious conservatives fear, the cultural trend toward their acceptance
will be reinforced, making it more likely that same-sex marriage will
eventually be legalized.

Civil Unions Are the Most Realistic Option

Nonetheless, such unions now represent the political center. They are
the safest territory to occupy. . . . At least some of those opposed to
same-sex marriage evidently think that civil unions provide a safe stop-
ping point, which buys off the gays and preserves marriage's character as an exclusively heterosexual institution. And some supporters of

> ## FAST FACT
>
> Civil unions, which are legal
> in Vermont, provide gay
> couples with the same
> rights and benefits as mar-
> ried people, including hos-
> pital visitation rights, access
> to medical information, sur-
> vivor benefits, spousal mili-
> tary benefits, adoption
> rights, and many others.

Gay marriage advocates make their voices heard at a Chicago rally in 2004. Civil unions are hailed by many as an ideal compromise to the gay marriage controversy.

same-sex marriage, myself among them, agree with the religious right that this is a step on the slippery slope to full marriage recognition. Consider the generational divide over same-sex marriage: while most Americans oppose it, most 18-to-29-year-olds are in favor. Perhaps this is why two-thirds of Americans think that same-sex marriage will eventually be legal in the United States. . . .

Civil unions are unstable compromises. They represent what the philosopher John Rawls disapprovingly called a "mere modus vivendi"—a compromise based not on principle, but on a contingent balance of political forces, which will be abandoned whenever those political forces happen to shift. Rawls is right to be unhappy about such compromises. It would be better to live in a society that is united at least on matters of political principle, if not on religion or the nature of the good life. But it is hard to see how that can happen any time soon with respect to same-sex marriage.

The same-sex marriage debate reveals the limits of community in modern America. Not only is it impossible for us to agree about marriage, we can't even agree on the principles that ought to govern the debate. Under these circumstances, the best hope for civil peace is to lower the stakes. . . .

In the long run, of course, civil unions can't be the solution. The resistance to them, particularly among the activists on both sides, is too great. But we live in the short run. Civil unions are the most politically stable answer for the next decade or so. Given the depth of our moral disagreement, that is saying a lot.

EVALUATING THE AUTHOR'S ARGUMENTS:

In the viewpoint you just read, author Andrew Koppelman suggests establishing civil unions as a compromise to gay marriage. If you were writing an essay on gay marriage, would you endorse this idea as a good solution to the problem? Why or why not? Explain your reasoning.

The Gay Community Does Not Need Marriage

Michael Bronski

In the following viewpoint, author Michael Bronski argues that homosexuals should not be interested in pursuing the right to marry because marriage limits one's personal freedom and sexual expression in a way that is antithetical to the gay liberation movement. He describes the origins of the gay rights movement, which viewed marriage as a flawed and confining institution that did not naturally mesh with the gay community's interest in equal rights, social justice, and alternative lifestyles. In the author's view, the current push for gay marriage has consumed the gay community to the point where it has forgotten its distaste for such traditional rites and is no longer thinking critically or creatively about how to solve more pressing problems. The author concludes that the gay community is compromising its identity by pushing for the right to marry and should not settle for acceptance into a tradition that offers it so little.

> *"Fighting for marriage is like fighting over yesterday's leftovers."*

Gay rights activist Michael Bronski is a frequent contributor to gay and lesbian magazines and literary journals. He is the author of *The Pleasure Principle: Sex, Backlash, and the Struggle for Gay Freedom* and *Pulp Friction: Uncovering the Golden Age of Gay Male Pulps.*

AS YOU READ, CONSIDER THE FOLLOWING QUESTIONS:
1. According to the author, what did the gay rights and feminist movements of the 1960s have in common?
2. Why do you think the author finds the fight for gay marriage "depressing"?
3. According to the author, what kinds of personal situations might cause gay people to not seek marriage?

Marriage rights mania is in the air. . . . The Pew Research Center reported [in Fall 2003] that 38 percent of those polled said they backed the idea of gay marriages, up 11 percent from [1996]. Meanwhile, an NBC/*Wall Street Journal* poll from November 1999 found that 66 percent of the public believes it's only a matter of time before queers win the right to marry.

All this should be good news for a queer activist like me, who's spent 35 years advocating for gay rights, right? Well, no. Let me explain.

Gay pride parades like this one in Hollywood are a legacy of the gay liberation movement. Traditionally, the movement has rejected the institution of marriage.

Many gay couples believe that obtaining the right to marry is not a necessary step in the fight for equal rights.

I've made a career out of political organizing and advocacy of gay and lesbian issues. I joined New York's Gay Liberation Front less than a month after the Stonewall riots[1] and I've been working on queer issues ever since. While I can appreciate why winning the right to marry will be seen as a bringing down the walls of a heterosexual Jericho, I also view it as a limited, very small "victory." . . .

Gay Liberation Is About Freedom and Alternatives

When the gay liberation movement formed in 1969, we had a broad, expansive vision of social justice. We wanted to change the world and make it better—not just for gay men and lesbians (this was before bisexuals and transgender people were fighting along with us), but for everyone. We wanted to find alternatives to the traditional structures under which we were raised, structures that many of us found insufficient to meet our needs and desires. We aligned ourselves with other movements and learned from them. We got "Gay Is Good" from the Black Power movement's "Black Is Beautiful." From the new feminist

1. a series of violent conflicts between homosexuals and police in New York City in 1969

movement, we learned that patriarchy—especially when it mandated compulsory heterosexuality—was as bad for queers as it was for women. We also believed, like many feminists, that marriage was, at its best, an imperfect institution, and, at its worst, a dangerous one. . . .

What feminists saw as the problem with marriage . . . was that marriage privatized intimate relationships, hindered community interaction, and regulated sexuality. The feminist critique of marriage sought to promote personal freedom and sexual liberation. It chafed against the notion that the only valid relationships were those that had been endorsed—and financially supported—by the state. The feminist critique of marriage, signed onto fully by the Gay Liberation Front, made clear that the state had no business telling us what we could do with our bodies (especially with regard to reproduction), what we could do in bed, or with whom we could do it. We understood that what the state allowed, or sanctioned, was in the state's interests, and not ours.

These were not crackpot ideas coming from the lunatic hippie fringe. They were at the center of a very lively public debate about the best ways for women and men to lead their personal and sexual lives. In 1970, Kate Millett's *Sexual Politics,* in which she seriously questioned the idea that marriage was necessary for personal happiness or the successful raising of children, was a *New York Times* bestseller. Other books—Shulamith Firestone's 1970 *The Dialectic of Sex: The Case for Feminist Revolution* and Dorothy Dinnerstein's 1976 *The Mermaid and the Minotaur: Human Malaise and Sexual Arrangements*—were widely discussed in the popular press. In 1971, Nena and George O'Neill published *Open Marriage,* a how-to guide for people who wanted to expand their ideas about intimate relationships. It sold over one million copies in less than a year. The culture was desperately hungry for alternatives to traditional sexual relationships. Ideas about communal living, extended non-biological families, and collective child-raising were also in the air.

FAST FACT

According to a Harris poll taken in March 2004, just 71 percent of all gay, lesbian, and bisexual people surveyed said that gay couples should be allowed to marry.

Nobody was saying, let's get rid of marriage, but they were extraordinarily interested in exploring alternatives to it. . . .

Marriage Is Too Stifling for the Gay Community

The problem with the current obsession among gay rights groups like the Human Rights Campaign and the National Gay and Lesbian Task Force is that marriage still poses the same problems it did in the late 1960s. Is this the best way for most people to organize their most intimate relationships and does marriage ultimately make people as happy and productive as they might otherwise be? Well, given the 50 percent divorce rate, the ongoing epidemic of domestic violence among straight and gay couples, and the number of people who seek marital counsel from the likes of [self-help psychologists] Dr. Phil, Dr. Laura, and Dr. Ruth—not to mention the vital role fantasies of conjugal cheating play on television and in Hollywood, I would have to conclude that marriage falls far short of its exalted reputation. . . .

There is nothing intrinsically wrong with queers buying in to the marriage myth—although it does strike me as odd, given that we have managed to do so well without it for so long. But the fight for marriage rights has become the elusive Holy Grail of gay freedom: when we are granted same-sex marriage, we will have achieved transcendent acceptance. In the early 1970s, we had continuous, vibrant community discussions about how best to enact the new freedoms we were discovering. In those years, we rejected myths embraced by earlier queer generations—that we had to be private to be safe, that our sexual desire was a form of mental illness, that we were doomed to hell, that we had to replicate the most staid heterosexual relationship patterns to have any chance at personal happiness. Rather, we thought we could create a better world, one more in tune with our needs and desires.

I hear very little discussion now—in the gay press or in our national organizations—about how queer people feel about marriage. Everyone agrees that gay people must have equality under the law, but do we hear from people who don't want to get married? From people who think their relationships are fine the way they are? From people who have found that monogamy doesn't work for them? From people who feel their lives have been seriously encumbered by having kids and being in a traditional relationship? From people who

Gays demonstrate pride in their sexual orientation by marching with an enormously long rainbow flag. Some activists argue that legalized gay marriage would greatly weaken the liberation movement.

chafe at the idea that under the traditional definition of marriage, monogamy is not only expected, but also mandated? . . .

Settling for Small Crumbs

Fighting for marriage is like fighting over yesterday's leftovers rather than coming up with something new and better. Even as we fight for the right to marry, there is still so much to do. We can't even pass a federal nondiscrimination bill, much less make the streets safe for transgender kids who are being murdered in their own neighborhoods. . . .

As an old-time gay liberationist, I find the frenzy around marriage organizing exciting, but depressing. I would never have imagined that a movement that started out in the bars, the streets, and in public cruising places could have come this far. The gay liberation movement had a vision of radical change and making the world a better place. Securing the right to marry will make the world a better place, but it will not change the world. It doesn't even change marriage. In the end, it is such a big fight for such a small gain.

In 1969, we didn't just want, as we said then, a piece of the pie. We wanted to take over the bakery and produce a huge array of tasty, extravagant, nutritious, luscious, and inviting foodstuffs for queers and everyone else. I don't think we ever imagined that our movement would one day be happy to settle for such small crumbs, no matter how sweet.

EVALUATING THE AUTHOR'S ARGUMENTS:

In the viewpoint you just read, author Michael Bronski, a homosexual with a long history of gay rights activism, argues against gay marriage. There are other social commentators who are also against gay marriage, but for very different reasons than Bronski. Considering what you know on this subject, what differences do you see between Bronski's argument and others? Does the fact that Bronski is gay influence the weight you give his argument? Why or why not? Explain your reasoning.

CHAPTER 2

How Should Marriage Be Legislated?

A man holds up a sign declaring that legislators should treat gay marriage as a fundamental human right.

VIEWPOINT

1

The Government Should Legislate Moral Issues

David Limbaugh

"Of course we can legislate morality. We always have. We must."

In the following viewpoint, author David Limbaugh argues prohibiting gay marriage is necessary to preserve and protect Americans' moral values. He contends that most American codes of behavior, such as systems of punishment, property ownership, law, and even the Constitution, are based on biblical concepts of morality. Therefore, to reject the idea that Judeo-Christian culture can be the foundation for a definition of marriage, as the author argues Massachusetts has done with its decision to legalize gay marriage, is to undermine the very foundations of American society. For these reasons, the author concludes that marriage must be defined as that between a man and a woman, and that in order for American society to successfully proceed it must embrace a culture based on biblical morality.

David Limbaugh is a syndicated columnist. His most recent book, *Persecution,* argues that Christians are increasingly persecuted and discriminated against in America.

David Limbaugh, "Uprooting Our Biblical Foundation," www.davidlimbaugh.com, November 21, 2003.

Given the public outcry about the federal court's order for the removal of Judge Roy Moore's Ten Commandments display, I'm surprised there isn't as much alarm about the [2003] Massachusetts Supreme Court decision to sanctify gay marriage.

In the Moore case you have a federal court telling a state court that it can't symbolically recognize the God of the Bible as the source of our laws (or otherwise). In the Massachusetts case you have a state court ruling that the Bible can't be the source of our laws. I think the latter has even graver implications.

A Dangerous Trend Away from Morality

Follow me on this. There is little question that the institution of marriage between a man and woman was ordained by the Bible.

Genesis 2:24 says, "Therefore shall a man leave his father and his mother, and shall cleave unto his wife: and they shall be one flesh." That is a prescription for man and woman to be joined, not man and man or woman and woman.

The Massachusetts court ruled that because the Massachusetts Constitution "affirms the dignity and equality of all individuals" and

> # FAST FACT
>
> Judeo-Christian ideas are woven throughout American society. American currency reads "In God We Trust," the pledge of allegiance refers to "One nation under God," and Bibles are used to ensure people's honesty in federal courtrooms.

The task of the Supreme Court (pictured in 2003) is to ensure the constitutionality of the nation's laws. Many Americans, however, feel that laws should be grounded in a moral code.

"forbids the creation of second-class citizens," homosexuals have a right to marry.

This should be no surprise, as it is a result of a logical progression in our jurisprudence toward radical individualism—the rights of the individual trump everything else—including the interest of the major-ity in establishing a moral and stable society.

Since the United States Supreme Court in its recent sodomy case (*Lawrence vs. Texas*) reaffirmed the Court's earlier pronouncement that "Our obligation is to define the liberty of all, not to mandate our own moral code," it's hardly a surprise that a state court is following suit. The Massachusetts court is doing precisely that: forbidding the state legisla-ture from mandating a moral code—at least one with Biblical roots.

Biblical Morality Guides Much of Our Culture

The oft-repeated lie that "we can't legislate morality" has finally born its poisonous fruits. Of course we can legislate morality. We always have. We must. Try looking at the criminal code of any state or the federal system and tell me it isn't based on morality. Look further into our civil law and try to deny that much, if not most, of tort law and contract law, not to mention property law, are rooted in our traditional (Biblical) moral beliefs.

Supporters celebrate the decision of the Massachusetts Supreme Court to allow gays to marry.
Many Americans condemn gay marriage, legal or not, as immoral.

Founding father John Adams claimed the Constitution was drafted exclusively for the benefit of moral and religious people.

It is not just for mercantile reasons that men are prohibited from breaching contracts. And punitive damages in tort law are awarded not to compensate the victim, but to punish the tortfeasor. Punishment—that's a moral concept.

Not only are our statutory and common law rooted in Biblical morality; at a more fundamental level, so is our Constitution. If we remove that foundation, the fabric of our society will unravel, and we'll eventually lose our liberties—ironically, at the hands of those claiming to champion freedom. And, by the way, the Massachusetts Supreme Court, in demolishing traditional marriage, is itself legislating—that's right, I said "legislating," not "adjudicating," morality.

Secularists in our culture and on our courts are not just turning the First Amendment Establishment Clause on its head and using it as a weapon to smother religious liberty for Christians. They are further attacking our Judeo-Christian foundation by promoting individualism to the extreme—to the exclusion of Biblical truths.

In the abortion cases, the mother's personal convenience taken to an obscene extreme trumps the very right to life of the baby made in God's image. In the Massachusetts gay marriage case, the Biblical concept of marriage is summarily and arrogantly rejected by four robed anti-culture warriors in favor of the newfound sanctification of homosexual behavior.

Our Culture Cannot Be Divorced from Its Roots

We might as well just be blunt about what's happened. According to our renegade courts, the government is not just forbidden from endorsing the Christian religion, it must now disavow its Judeo-Christian heritage. It must bastardize itself.

Sadly, chillingly, it's all based on a lie: that the Framers [of the Constitution] intended to create an impregnable wall of separation between religion and government. But whatever the Framers believed, they certainly didn't intend to bastardize government from its Biblical parentage the instant it was spawned. What sense would it have made for them to build our Constitution on the solid, immovable rock of Biblical principles, then immediately uproot that foundational anchor?

The courts are making quite clear their disenchantment with this wonderful document we call our Constitution, as they dismantle it bit by bit. If the prescient John Adams was correct that our Constitution is made only for a moral and religious people, perhaps before too long it will not be suitable for us.

EVALUATING THE AUTHORS' ARGUMENTS:

In the viewpoint you just read, the author argues that it is acceptable for government to adopt a definition of gay marriage based on religious morals. In the following viewpoint, the author argues that government's definition of marriage should not have any ties to religion. After reading both viewpoints, which argument do you find more compelling? Why?

The Government Should Not Legislate Moral Issues

Howard Moody

"If marriage is . . . a major contributor to the social order in our society, why would anyone want to shut out homosexuals from the 'glorious attributes' of this 'sacred institution'"?

In the following viewpoint, author Reverend Howard Moody argues that the debate over gay marriage is a debate about the separation of church and state. The author contends that the state's current definition of marriage is thoroughly intertwined with religious definitions of marriage and therefore violates the American principle that church and state should be kept separate. He describes civil, or state, marriage as that which is supposed to simply regulate the voluntary pairing of two individuals for whatever purposes they see fit. Romantic, mystical, or other meanings of marriage are imparted by religious institutions, and such values do not belong in the state. Therefore, the author concludes that if church and state are to be properly separated on the issue of marriage, the United States must legalize same-sex marriage.

Howard Moody is minister emeritus of Judson Memorial Church in New York City.

Howard Moody, "Gay Marriage Shows Why We Need to Separate Church and State," *The Nation,* July 5, 2004.
Copyright © 2004 by The Nation Magazine/The Nation Company, Inc. Reproduced by permission.

AS YOU READ, CONSIDER THE FOLLOWING QUESTIONS:
1. According to the author, what should have provoked an outcry from clergy around the country?
2. When the author presides over weddings, why does he refrain from saying, "by the authority invested in me by the State of New York"?
3. In what ways does the author consider President Bush both right and wrong about his convictions regarding marriage?

We are now in the midst of a national debate on the nature of marriage, and it promises to be as emotional and polemical as the issues of abortion and homosexuality have been over the past century. What all these debates have in common is that they involved both the laws of the state and the theology of the church. The purpose of this writing is to suggest that the gay-marriage debate is less about the legitimacy of the loving relationship of a same-sex couple than about the relationship of church and state and how they define marriage. . . .

Marriage, Religion and the State

In order to fully understand the conflict that has arisen in this debate over the nature of marriage, it is important to understand the difference between the religious definition of marriage and the state's secular and civil definition. The government's interest is in a legal definition of marriage—a social and voluntary contract between a man and woman in order to protect money, property and children. Marriage is a civil union without benefit of clergy or religious definition. The state is not interested in why two people are "tying the knot," whether it's to gain money, secure a dynasty or raise children. It may be hard for those of us who have a religious or romantic view of marriage to realize that loveless marriages are not that rare. Before the [birth control] Pill, pregnancy was a frequent motive for getting married. The state doesn't care what the commitment of two people is, whether it's for life or as long as both of you love, whether it's sexually monogamous or an open marriage. There is nothing

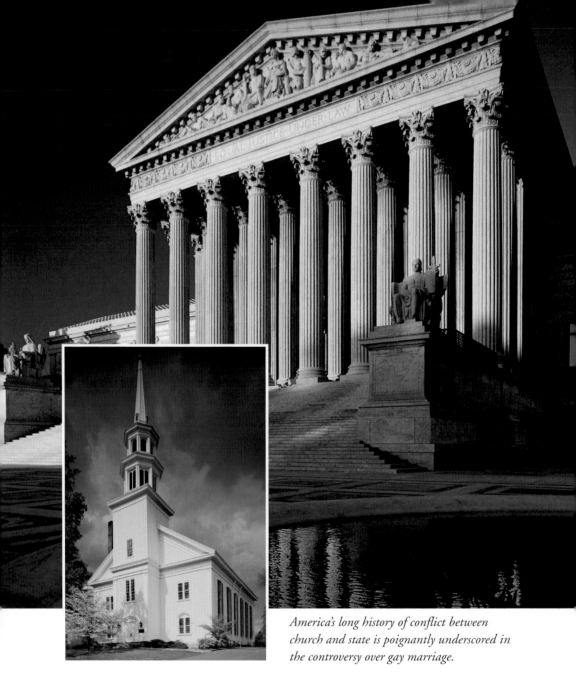

America's long history of conflict between church and state is poignantly underscored in the controversy over gay marriage.

spiritual, mystical or romantic about the state's license to marry—it's a legal contract.

Thus, [President] George W. Bush is right when he says that "marriage is a sacred institution" when speaking as a Christian, as a member of his Methodist church. But as President of the United States and leader of all Americans, believers and unbelievers, he is wrong. What will surface in this debate as litigation and court decisions multiply is the history of the conflict between the church and the state in defining the nature of marriage. That history will become significant as we move toward a decision on who may be married.

After Christianity became the state religion of the Roman Empire in A.D. 325, the church maintained absolute control over the regulation of marriage for some 1,000 years. Beginning in the sixteenth century,

In 2000 California voters approved Proposition 22, which defined marriage as a union between a man and a woman for legal purposes in that state.

English kings (especially Henry VIII, who found the inability to get rid of a wife extremely oppressive) and other monarchs in Europe began to wrest control from the church over marital regulations. Ever since, kings, presidents and rulers of all kinds have seen how important the control of marriage is to the regulation of social order. In the United States, the government has always been in charge of marriage. . . .

In the sixteenth century, English king Henry VIII wrested control of marriage from the church.

The civil law view of marriage has as much historical diversity as the church's own experience because, in part, the church continued to influence the civil law. Although it was the Bible that made "the husband the head of his wife," it was common law that "turned the married pair legally into one person—the husband," as Nancy Cott documents in her book *Public Vows: A History of Marriage and the Nation* (an indispensable resource for anyone seeking to understand the changing nature of marriage in the nation's history). She suggests that "the legal doctrine of marital unity was called coverture . . . [which] meant that the wife could not use legal avenues such as suits or contracts, own assets, or execute legal documents without her husband's collaboration." This view of the wife would not hold water in any court in the land today.

As a matter of fact, even in the religious understanding

of President Bush and his followers, allowing same-sex couples the right to marry seems a logical conclusion. If marriage is "the most fundamental institution of civilization" and a major contributor to the social order in our society, why would anyone want to shut out homosexuals from the "glorious attributes" of this "sacred institution"? Obviously, the only reason one can discern is that the opponents believe that gay and lesbian people are not worthy of the benefits and spiritual blessings of "marriage."

We Must Enforce Separation of Church and State

At the heart of the controversy raging over same-sex marriage is the religious and constitutional principle of the separation of church and state. All of us can probably agree that there was never a solid wall of separation, riddled as it is with breaches. The evidence of that is seen in the ambiguity of tax-free religious institutions, "in God we trust" printed on our money and "under God" in the Pledge of Allegiance to our country. All of us clergy, who are granted permission by the state to officiate at legal marriage ceremonies, have already compromised the "solid wall" by signing the license issued by the state. I would like to believe that my authority to perform religious ceremonies does not come from the state but derives from the vows of ordination and my commitment to God. I refuse to repeat the words, "by the authority invested in me by the State of New York, I pronounce you husband and wife," but by signing the license, I've become the state's "handmaiden."

It seems fitting therefore that we religious folk should now seek to sharpen the difference between ecclesiastical law [that is, religious law] and civil law as we beseech the state to clarify who can be married by civil law. Further evidence that the issue of church and state is part of the gay-marriage controversy is that two Unitarian ministers have been arrested for solemnizing unions between same-sex couples when no

> ## FAST FACT
>
> The U.S. Supreme Court has interpreted the intent of the First Amendment to preserve a separation between church and state. This means that no government may officially adopt a particular religion or religious ideology, and government must avoid excessive involvement in religious matters.

A Methodist minister officiates a lesbian couple's wedding in San Francisco City Hall, adding a religious element to their civil ceremony.

state licenses were involved. Ecclesiastical law may punish those clergy who disobey marital regulations, but the state has no right to invade church practices and criminalize clergy under civil law. There should have been a noisy outcry from all churches, synagogues and mosques at the government's outrageous contravention of the sacred principle of the "free exercise of religion."

Regardless of Our Religious Views

I come from a long line of Protestants who believe in a "free church in a free state." In the issue before this nation, the civil law is the determinant of the regulation of marriage, regardless of our religious views, and the Supreme Court will finally decide what the principle of equality means in our Constitution in the third century of our life together as a people. It is likely that the Commonwealth of Massachusetts will probably lead the nation on this matter, as the State of New York led to the Supreme Court decision to allow women reproductive freedom. . . .

In time, and I believe that time is now, we Americans will see that all the fears foisted on us by religious zealots were not real. Heterosexual marriage will still flourish with its statistical failures. The only difference will be that some homosexual couples will join them and probably account for about the same number of failed relationships. And we will discover that it did not matter whether the couples were joined in a religious ceremony or a secular and civil occasion for the statement of their intentions.

EVALUATING THE AUTHORS' ARGUMENTS:

The authors of the viewpoints you just read are both religious men. David Limbaugh is a Christian who has written extensively in defense of Christian values and traditions. Howard Moody is a Protestant minister who has served as a clergyman for over thirty years. Yet they disagree over the role religion should play in civil society. After reading their opinions on the matter, what role do you believe religion should play in civil society? Does your position on this issue influence your opinion on whether gay marriage should be legalized or banned? Explain your answer.

Gay Marriage Should Be Left to the States

Jonathan Rauch

"On certain social issues . . . people don't agree and probably never will— and the single political advantage of the federalist system is that they don't have to."

Jonathan Rauch is a correspondent for *Atlantic Monthly,* from which this viewpoint was taken. He is also the author of *Gay Marriage: Why It Is Good for Gays, Good for Straights, and Good for America.* In the following viewpoint, Rauch argues that gay marriage should be neither federally banned nor mandated; instead, states should be able to rule individually on the issue. He suggests that America's federalist system is well equipped to handle problems in which Americans disagree on how a particular issue should be legislated. He points out that states have differing laws on other complicated issues, such as banking, ownership of property, and product standards, and sees no reason why gay marriage should not be legal in the states that want it and illegal in the states that do not. This is the best solution to the debate over same-sex marriage, Rauch argues, because it is unrealistic to think that the entire nation will ever be able to agree on certain issues. He concludes that the federalist system is precisely set up to handle these types of problems and should be used to settle the debate over same-sex marriage.

AS YOU READ, CONSIDER THE FOLLOWING QUESTIONS:
1. What do you think the author means when he says that the states are "laboratories for democracy"?
2. At the end of the article, the author uses the analogy of a loaf of bread to mean what?
3. According to the author, what is the relationship between America's diversity and its federalist system?

L ast November [2003] the Supreme Judicial Court of Massachusetts ruled that excluding gay couples from civil marriage violated the state constitution. The court gave the legislature six months—until May [2004]—to do something about it. Some legislators mounted efforts to amend the state constitution to ban same-sex marriage, but as of this writing they have failed (and even if passed, a ban would not take effect until at least 2006). With unexpected urgency the country faces the possibility that marriage licenses might

Demonstrators in Boston rally against a state constitutional amendment to ban gay marriage. Some argue that state legislatures, not Congress, should decide the issue.

THE CONSTITUTION
DEFEND IT
don't amend it

soon be issued to homosexual couples. To hear the opposing sides talk, a national culture war is unavoidable.

But same-sex marriage neither must nor should be treated as an all-or-nothing national decision. Instead individual states should be left to try gay marriage if and when they choose—no national ban, no national mandate. Not only would a decentralized approach be in keeping with the country's most venerable legal traditions; it would also improve, in three ways, the odds of making same-sex marriage work for gay and straight Americans alike.

The Benefits of Allowing States to Choose

First, it would give the whole country a chance to learn. Nothing terrible—in fact, nothing even noticeable—seems to have happened to marriage since Vermont began allowing gay civil unions, in 2000. But civil unions are not marriages. The only way to find out what would happen if same-sex couples got marriage certificates is to let some of us do it. Turning marriage into a nationwide experiment might be rash, but trying it in a few states would provide test cases on a smaller scale. Would the divorce rate rise? Would the marriage rate fall? We should get some indications before long. Moreover, states are, as the saying goes, the laboratories of democracy. One state might opt for straightforward legalization. Another might add some special provisions (for instance, regarding child custody or adoption). A third might combine same-sex marriage with counseling or other assistance (not out of line with a growing movement to offer social-service support to so-called fragile families). Variety would help answer some important questions: Where would gay marriage work best? What kind of community support would it need? What would be the avoidable pitfalls? Either to forbid same-sex marriage nationwide or to legalize it nationwide would be to throw away a wealth of potential information.

Just as important is the social benefit of letting the states find their own way. Law is only part of what gives marriage its binding power; community support and social expectations are just as important. In a community that looked on same-sex marriage with bafflement or hostility, a gay couple's marriage certificate while providing legal benefits, would confer no social support from the heterosexual majority.

Many heterosexuals, like the couple on the right, support gay marriage. Enabling states to rule on the issue of gay marriage would ensure that diverse opinions are taken into account.

Both the couple and the community would be shortchanged. Letting states choose gay marriage wouldn't guarantee that everyone in the state recognized such marriages as legitimate, but it would pretty well ensure that gay married couples could find some communities in their state that did.

Finally, the political benefit of a state-by-state approach is not to be underestimated. This is the benefit of avoiding a national culture war.

States Can and Should Go Their Own Way

The United States is not (thank goodness) a culturally homogeneous country. It consists of many distinct moral communities. On certain social issues, such as abortion and homosexuality, people don't agree and probably never will—and the single political advantage of the federalist system is that they don't have to. Individuals and groups who find the values or laws of one state obnoxious have the right to live somewhere else. . . .

So well suited is the federalist system to the gay-marriage issue that it might almost have been set up to handle it. . . .

Marriage laws (and, of course, divorce laws) continue to be established by the states. They differ on many points, from age of consent to who may marry whom. In Arizona, for example, first cousins are allowed to marry only if both are sixty-five or older or the couple can prove to a judge "that one of the cousins is unable to reproduce." (So much for the idea that marriage is about procreation.) Conventional wisdom notwithstanding, the Constitution does not require states to recognize one another's marriages. . . . If Delaware, for example, decided to lower its age of consent to ten, no other state would be required to regard a ten-year-old as legally married. The public-policy excep-

Historically, the laws of individual states have agreed on a conventional definition of marriage as a lawful union between one man and one woman.

tion, as it is called, is only common sense. If each state could legislate for all the rest, American-style federalism would be at an end.

Why, then, do the states all recognize one another's marriages? Because they choose to. Before the gay-marriage controversy arose, the country enjoyed a general consensus on the terms of marriage. Interstate differences were so small that states saw no need to split hairs, and mutual recognition was a big convenience. The issue of gay marriage, of course, changes the picture, by asking states to reconsider an accepted boundary of marriage. This is just the sort of controversy in which the Founders imagined that individual states could and often should go their separate ways. . . .

States Differ on Many Types of Law

Is a state-by-state approach impractical and unsustainable? Possibly, but the time to deal with any problems is if and when they arise. Going in, there is no reason to expect any great difficulty. There are many precedents for state-by-state action. The country currently operates under a tangle of different state banking laws. As any banker will tell you, the lack of uniformity has made interstate banking more difficult. But we do have interstate banks. Bankers long ago got used to meeting different requirements in different states. Similarly, car manufacturers have had to deal with zero-emission rules in California and a few other states. Contract law, property law, and criminal law all vary significantly from state to state. Variety is the point of federalism. Uniform national policies may be convenient, but they risk sticking us with the same wrong approach everywhere.

My guess is that if one or two states allowed gay marriage, a confusing transitional period, while state courts and legislatures worked out what to do, would quickly lead in all but a few places to routines that everyone

> **FAST FACT**
>
> Marriage has historically been a matter that is adjudicated on a state-by-state basis. The U.S. Supreme Court has interfered in state laws regarding marriage just twice—to require Utah to ban the practice of polygamy in the nineteenth century, and to force sixteen states to legalize interracial marriage in 1967.

Just Married!

Allowing states to decide on the issue would allow gay couples like this one to continue clinging to the hope that their unions will one day be officially recognized.

would soon take for granted. If New Jersey adopted gay marriage, for instance, New York would have a number of options. It might refuse to recognize the marriages. It might recognize them. It might honor only certain aspects of them—say, medical power of attorney, or inheritance and tenancy rights. A state with a civil-union or domestic-partner law might automatically confer that law's benefits on any gay couple who got married in New Jersey. My fairly confident expectation is that initially most states would reject out-of-state gay marriages (as, indeed, most states have pre-emptively done), but a handful would fully accept them, and others would choose an intermediate option. . . .

Letting the States Rule Is a Good Compromise

If you are starving, one or two slices of bread may not be as good as a loaf—but it is far better than no bread at all. The damage that exclusion from marriage has done to gay lives and gay culture comes not just from being unable to marry right now and right here but from knowing the law forbids us ever to marry at all. The first time a state adopted same-sex marriage, gay life would change forever. The full benefits would come only when same-sex marriage was legal everywhere. But gay people's lives would improve with the first state's announcement that in this community, marriage is open to everyone.

EVALUATING THE AUTHOR'S ARGUMENTS:

In the viewpoint you just read, author Jonathan Rauch proposes that the controversy over same-sex marriage be settled by letting each state decide its own position on gay marriage. Considering what you know on this topic, do you think this is a fair compromise for both supporters and opponents of gay marriage? Why or why not? Use examples from the text to illustrate your point.

Prohibiting Gay Marriage Violates Civil Rights

Victoria A. Brownworth

"The fight for queer civil rights is as important to the 21st century as the fight for black civil rights was to the 20th."

In the following viewpoint, author Victoria A. Brownworth argues that denying gay couples the right to marry infringes on their civil rights to life, liberty, and the pursuit of happiness. She contends that when an entire group of people is denied the opportunity to participate in an aspect of society, they are relegated to second-class citizens. Moreover, that gays are denied the right to marry precludes them from other important legal rights that come with marriage, such as tax benefits and inheritance rights. She compares the struggle for gay rights to the black civil rights movement of the 1960s, where blacks, through important acts of civil disobedience, overcame institutionalized discrimination that relegated them second-class citizens. The author concludes by stating it is wrong to deny any group of Americans their civil rights and that gay Americans and their supporters must be undeterred in their fight for equality and justice.

An award-winning and Pulitzer Prize–nominated journalist, Victoria A. Brownworth's articles have appeared in *Ms.*, the *Nation*, the *Village Voice*, the *Philadelphia Daily News*, and *Curve*, the journal from which this viewpoint was taken. She is also the author of seven books, including *Too Queer: Essays from a Radical Life*.

AS YOU READ, CONSIDER THE FOLLOWING QUESTIONS:

1. Why do you think the author shares her personal memories of protesting during the 1960s' civil rights movement? Do you think this technique helps strengthen her argument?
2. What point is the author trying to make by raising the issue of Jews and Nazis, and apartheid in South Africa?
3. According to the author, in what ways are the gay rights movement and the black civil rights movement of the 1960s similar?

I t began back in February [2004]. The newly elected Democratic mayor of San Francisco, Gavin Newsom, decided to issue marriage licenses to lesbians and gay men and perform marriage ceremonies at San Francisco City Hall. Within weeks, several other communities were doing it as well, in New Mexico and New York. By March [2004], it was happening in Arizona and New Jersey. Now, in May [2004], queer marriages may be happening—with full legal rights attached—in Massachusetts, where the fight began in earnest when the Massachusetts State Supreme Court stipulated in a January [2004] ruling that to deny lesbians and gay men the full rights of legal marriage would violate that state's constitution.

President [George W.] Bush called the San Francisco marriages "troubling" and attributed the Massachusetts ruling to "activist judges trying to overturn the basic fabric of American society." In February [2004], the president called for a constitutional amendment banning marriages between anyone other than one man and one woman. . . .

> **FAST FACT**
>
> The last of the laws preventing people of different races from marrying each other was overturned in 1967 in a case known as *Loving v. Virginia*.

Some gay couples that obtained marriage licenses in 2004, like these men walking from San Francisco City Hall with their adopted twins, thought of themselves as participants in acts of civil disobedience.

For conservatives, queer marriage has become the litmus test abortion once was, defining a [religious] cultural perspective on American politics. For liberals, queer marriage has become the proving ground for just how liberal they are: As the old 1960s axiom queried about race, "Yes, but would you want your daughter to marry one?"

Fortunately, many liberals are recognizing that the fight for queer civil rights is as important to the 21st century as the fight for black civil rights was to the 20th.

A New Civil-Rights Movement

When I was a child, my parents were deeply involved in the black civil-rights movement, and they engaged in numerous acts of civil disobedience. In high school, I was deeply involved in the anti-war movement protesting American engagement in Vietnam and Cambodia. I was arrested repeatedly for acts of protest and civil disobedience. I was arrested again for acts of civil disobedience in the 1980s, when I became involved with ACT UP and other groups in the AIDS movement.

My parents were not black. I was not in danger of being drafted. Nor was I HIV-positive. Yet my parents and I fought in political movements that were not tied directly to our personal identity, because we wanted to work for what was right.

The people—mayors, judges, city clerks—who have chosen to step outside their conscripted purview as political figures and help marry their queer constituents, in the face of strong opposition and even presidential censure, are engaged in important acts of civil disobedience. They have become freedom riders in a new civil-rights movement, the one that will eventually be responsible for granting full citizenship to American queers.

Civil Rights Are Won by Many

We cannot overstate the importance of these acts of civil disobedience, nor the importance of civil disobedience as a tool in the quest for equality and civil rights. We cannot overstate the impact of straight Americans like Gavin Newsom who risk political suicide, even arrest, for what is right.

Source: Siers. © 2003 by *The Charlotte Observer*. Reproduced by permission of North America Syndicate.

I was fortunate to grow up in a socialist-political household with parents who had strong convictions about justice and equality. Growing up in that atmosphere, stuffing envelopes and making signs for marches, fending off the chants of "nigger lover" at school, watching my parents being threatened by members of the KKK [Klu Klux Klan] and other racist groups, I learned valuable lessons about why one must do what is morally right, even if it isn't about us, per se: because it could be about us one day.

No civil-rights movement in the world has ever been fomented, led and actualized solely by the group it was meant to benefit. The lives of Jews and others targeted by the Nazis could not have been saved without the participation of "righteous Gentiles" who risked their lives

San Francisco mayor Gavin Newsom (left) risked political suicide when he supported legalized gay marriage in the city in 2004.

Thousands of protesters, black and white, take part in a 1963 civil rights demonstration. As a civil rights issue, gay marriage needs broad-based support if it is to be legalized.

to save others. Murderous apartheid in South Africa could not have ended without white Afrikaans prime minister Pieter Botha deciding to no longer participate in the process. Civil rights for blacks in the United States would not have been won without white Americans risking their lives for the freedom of black Americans. And civil rights will not be won for queer Americans without the participation of straights in the movement for our equal rights.

A Violation of My Civil Rights

I am not a proponent of marriage. I cringe at Kelli Carpenter and Tammy Lynn taking Rosie O'Donnell's and Melissa Etheridge's last names after their weddings like 1950s straight women, as if they no longer had their own names and identities. I would rather see the institution of marriage, which has damaged women irreparably in every country in the world and continues to do so in many nations today, dissolved completely. But in 2004 America, every heterosexual citizen

Source: Kirk. © 1996 by Kirk Anderson. Reproduced by permission.

is granted rights I am not privy to simply by virtue of her or his sexual orientation. I have friends in the United States who have been prevented from living with their lovers because those women are not American citizens. Thus, they cannot legally marry those women as they could if they were straight, and keep their lovers here.

That is wrong. That is unjust. That is a violation of my civil rights as an American citizen and the rights of my friends as American citizens. We should all have the option of marrying the person we love. . . .

The very first couple to be married in San Francisco were lesbian activists Del Martin, 83, and Phyllis Lyon, 79, who have been together for 51 years. These women have defied all odds and remained together for over half a century. Finally, after wanting to do so for decades, they were able to marry each other. How could that possibly infringe on anyone else's rights, in marriage or otherwise?

Our lives should not be in the hands of the straight majority any more than the lives of black Americans should have been in the hands of white Americans. But when the U.S. Supreme Court ruled against racial segregation in 1954 and against discrimination against queers in 2003,[1] civil-rights movements long in process took a giant leap forward.

---

1. The author is referring to a U.S. Supreme Court decision to legalize sodomy, or sex between two men.

The Time Is Now

We are fortunate that there are straight people of conscience who support our quest for civil rights. We are fortunate that we live in a nation where civil disobedience is a protected form of protest and that no one has been killed for supporting our cause.

But as we celebrate this [year's] Pride [a festival celebrating homosexuality], we must remember all those queers who lived in the shadows with no support, unable to voice their own identity, let alone declare it at their local city hall. There is a synergy to civil-rights movements, and the momentum is here now, with us.

We must urge all who are sympathetic to us, all those who love us and our families, to keep supporting our quest for civil rights. Write to your local leaders and demand to know why they too are not supporting us. Cite all those who have—both in past civil-rights movements and today in this one.

"Liberty and justice for all" means just that. Please remind those who run your country, state, city and town that you, too, have a vote. And you intend to vote for civil rights—your own and everyone else's.

EVALUATING THE AUTHOR'S ARGUMENTS:

In the viewpoint you just read, the author argues that gay couples should be given the right to marry, but she also writes, "I am not a proponent of marriage." What do you think the author means by these seemingly contradictory statements? Explain your answer.

Gay Marriage Is Not a Civil Rights Issue

Jeff Jacoby

"[Homosexuals] have not been deprived of the right to marry—only of the right to insist that a single-sex union is a 'marriage.'"

In the following viewpoint, author Jeff Jacoby argues that gay marriage is not a civil rights issue because homosexuals are not being denied their rights. He argues that the gay movement's comparison to the black civil rights movement of the 1960s is invalid because blacks sought to achieve the same exact rights and services that white Americans did. Gay Americans, however, are not excluded from the tradition of marriage; they may marry a person of the opposite sex any time they choose. The author argues that because gay Americans seek to reinvent the tradition of marriage and apply it to themselves, their cause is outside the realm of civil rights. Moreover, the author points out that the civil rights movement is based on the idea that God created all people equal. But integral to this idea is that God created men and women for holy matrimony. If gay activists deny that God created marriage as between a man and a woman, then they also have to deny he created all people as equal. Therefore, the author concludes that excluding same-sex unions from the tradition of marriage is not a violation of civil rights or justice; it upholds the natural limits of the institution as they have always existed.

Jeff Jacoby is a columnist for the *Boston Globe,* from which this viewpoint was taken.

AS YOU READ, CONSIDER THE FOLLOWING QUESTIONS:
1. According to the author, why have gay rights activists chosen to compare themselves to the civil rights movement?
2. What differences does the author see in the actions of the four college students seeking service at Woolworth's and the actions of gay and lesbian San Franciscans seeking marriage licenses?
3. What do you think the author means when he charges that gay activists are seeking to change the law "undemocratically"?

Homosexual marriage is not a civil rights issue. But that hasn't stopped the advocates of same-sex marriage from draping themselves in the glory of the civil rights movement—and smearing the defenders of traditional marriage as the moral equal of segregationists.

In *The New York Times* last Sunday [February 29, 2004], cultural critic Frank Rich, quoting a "civil rights lawyer," beatified the gay and lesbian couples lining up to receive illegal marriage licenses from San Francisco's new mayor, Gavin Newsom:

"An act as unremarkable as getting a wedding license has been transformed by the people embracing it, much as the unremarkable act of sitting at a Formica lunch counter was transformed by an act of civil disobedience at a Woolworth's [department store] in North Carolina 44 years ago this month." Nearby, the *Times* ran a photograph of a smiling lesbian couple in matching wedding veils—and an even larger photograph of a 1960 lunch counter sit-in.

Rich's essay—"The Joy of Gay Marriage"—went on to cast the supporters of traditional marriage as hateful zealots. They are "eager to foment the bloodiest culture war possible," he charged. "They are gladly donning the roles played by [segregationalist governors] Lester Maddox and George Wallace in the civil rights era."

But it is the marriage radicals like Rich and Newsom who are doing their best to inflame a culture war. And as is so often the case in wartime, truth—in this case, historical truth—has been an early casualty.

Civil Rights Sought to Restore Equality

For contrary to what Rich seems to believe, when Ezell Blair Jr., David Richmond, Joseph McNeil, and Franklin McCain approached the

Scores of gay couples line up outside San Francisco City Hall to obtain marriage licenses. A 2004 New York Times *editorial hailed these couples as the vanguard of a new civil rights movement.*

In 1963 a group of young blacks stages a sit-in to demand service at a whites-only lunch counter in a Woolworth's in Little Rock, Arkansas.

lunch counter of the Elm Street Woolworth's in Greensboro, N.C., on Feb. 1, 1960, all they asked for was a bite to eat. The four North Carolina Agricultural & Technical College students only wanted what any white customer might want, and *on precisely the same terms*—the same food at the same counter at the same price.

Those first four sit-in strikers, like the thousands of others who would emulate them at lunch counters across the South, weren't demanding that Woolworth's prepare or serve their food in ways it had never been prepared or served before. They weren't trying to do something that had never been lawful in any state of the union. They weren't bent on forcing a revolutionary change upon a timeless social institution.

All they were seeking was what should already have been theirs under the law of the land. The 14th Amendment had declared that blacks no less than whites were entitled to equal protection of the law. The Civil Rights Act of 1875 had barred discrimination in public accommodations.

But the Supreme Court had gutted those protections with shameful decisions in 1883 and 1896. The court's betrayal of black Americans was the reason why, more than six decades later, segregation still polluted so much of the nation. To restore the 14th Amendment to its original purpose, to re-create the Civil Rights Act, to return to black citizens the equality that had been stolen from them—that was the great cause of civil rights.

Gay Activists Seek to Change Reality

The marriage radicals, on the other hand, seek to restore nothing. They have not been deprived of the right to marry—only of the right to insist that a single-sex union is a "marriage." They cloak their demands in the language of civil rights because it sounds so much better than the truth: They don't want to accept or reject marriage on the same terms that it is available to everyone else. They want it on entirely new terms. They want it to be given a meaning it has never before had, and they prefer that it be done undemocratically—by judicial fiat, for example, or by mayors flouting the law. Whatever else that may be, it isn't civil rights. But dare to speak against it, and you are no better than [1960s Alabama police commissioner] Bull Connor [who ordered dogs and water hoses to be turned on crowds demonstrating for civil rights].

Fast Fact

According to a Harris poll taken in March 2004, 47 percent of Americans believed that denying same-sex couples the right to marry was not a violation of the principle that all people should be treated equally.

[In 2004], as Massachusetts lawmakers prepared to debate a constitutional amendment on the meaning of marriage, the state's leading black clergy came out strongly in support of the age-old definition: the union of a man and a woman. They were promptly tarred as enemies of civil rights. [Civil rights icon] "Martin Luther King," one left-wing [liberal] legislator barked, "is rolling over in his grave at a statement like this."

In 2004 these black church leaders in Georgia publicly declared that same-sex marriage is not a civil rights issue.

But if anything has King spinning in his grave, it is the indecency of exploiting his name for a cause he never supported. The civil rights movement for which he lived and died was grounded in a fundamental truth: All God's children are created equal. The same-sex marriage movement, by contrast, is grounded in the *denial* of a fundamental truth: The Creator who made us equal made us male and female. That duality has always and everywhere been the starting point for marriage. To claim that marriage can ignore that duality is akin to the claim, back when lunch counters were segregated, that America was a land of liberty and justice for all.

EVALUATING THE AUTHORS' ARGUMENTS:

The authors of the preceding articles each reach different conclusions on whether gay marriage constitutes a civil rights issue. If you were to write an article on gay marriage and civil rights, which position would you take? What evidence from these viewpoints would you use to make your argument?

CHAPTER 3

Does Gay Marriage Threaten Society?

Some people argue that extending the right to marry to gay couples represents a threat to society.

Gay Unions Threaten Society

Robert W. Patterson

In the following viewpoint, Robert W. Patterson argues that gay marriage threatens society because it does not positively serve the common good in the way that heterosexual marriages do. He contends that a stable society begins with the family, and that people get married in order to better their friends, family, and community and to successfully raise children, who will in turn benefit the community. Gay couples seeking marriage, however, are focused entirely on their own needs and what legal benefits they can incur from the state. Children can only artificially be part of this arrangement, and even when they are, their development, and thus the community's development, are in jeopardy. Furthermore, the author argues that homosexual relationships are primarily about passion and lust, which destabilizes society and victimizes women and children. The author concludes that gay marriage must be banned in order to preserve social stability.

Robert W. Patterson is a research fellow of the Howard Center for Family, Religion, and Society in Rockford, Illinois. He is also contributing editor of the center's "New Research" publication.

"Gay marriage . . . does not and cannot serve the common good."

AS YOU READ, CONSIDER THE FOLLOWING QUESTIONS:
  1. What point is the author trying to make by raising the case of Episcopalian bishop Eugene Robinson?
  2. What does the author mean when he says that gay couples have children at "the expense of others"?
  3. If you were to write an essay on how gay marriage threatens society, what evidence might you use from this article?

"If any man can show any just cause why they may not lawfully be joined together, let him now speak, or else hereafter forever hold his peace."

—*Book of Common Prayer*

Not very long ago, ordained ministers posed this proposition to congregations early in weddings just before addressing the bride and groom about their intentions of becoming husband and wife. That most clergy today leave it out of wedding liturgies is unfortunate, as the question reflects a critical understanding of marriage largely lost on Americans today and especially upon those seeking civil recognition of same-sex couples.

Unions Must Benefit Society

The fact that a minister, functioning as an agent of the state, would seek approval of a marriage from parties other than the couple is revealing. That solicited confirmation expresses the reality that marriage is not just a legal contract between two individuals but also a dynamic relationship that, according to social historian Allan C. Carlson, stands at the core of a complex web of social bonds that begins with the couple, finds support from their respective families and extended kin, and extends to society at large. When family and friends assent to a marriage, they are judging the union good for *society*, not just good for the couple. In fact, this approbation is also granted on behalf of the future children that all related parties anticipate will naturally flow from such union.

This communal dimension is virtually nonexistent when it comes to same-sex relationships, evidence that such relationships should never be deemed equivalent to, or even an alternative to, marriage.

Source: Stayskal. © by Tribune Media Services. Reproduced by permission.

Unlike marriage, same-sex relationships are static, self-focused, and center almost exclusively on what the relationship delivers for the two partners, not what it represents to the supportive families or to society. Does a homosexual partner even solicit the blessing of his prospective partner's family? Do his aunts and uncles travel cross-country to celebrate the occasion? Who are the third parties to these pairings? Rarely conducted in a community setting like a church or synagogue, these newfangled arrangements are essentially private affairs with no organic ties to anything. Ironically, this private identity is praised by advocates like [writer] Andrew Sullivan who assert that gay marriage can't possibly impact the traditional marriages of others because it concerns only the two persons involved.

Gay Marriage Does Not Serve the Common Good

This narrow focus on the couple dominates even the campaign for legal recognition of gay marriage or civil unions. It's all about them. The stated justifications for same-sex marriage have nothing to do with how this approach to mating can contribute to the common good, but everything to do with what society can, or must, do for the couple. They seek health insurance, survivor benefits, and hospital visitation rights (even though no law prevents these things now). They demand these "benefits" and other "rights," the legal side effects that accrue to marriage that are rarely on the table when a man and woman decide to wed.

As every husband and wife knows, the real benefits of marriage are not technical legalities conferred upon it by an outside party, in this case the state, but are generated from within the institution itself—children, and eventually grandchildren. Nevertheless, because homosexual relationships are by definition sterile—because they cannot produce what really matters—their demands extend to finagling with biology or exploiting the brokenness of failed heterosexual relationships to "have" children, again at the expense of others.

Women and Children Are Victims of Gay Marriage

The tragedy of the celebrated [homosexual] Episcopal bishop, Eugene Robinson, vividly illustrates how homosexual relationships fall short of common good. His decision more than ten years ago to enter into a "relationship" with another man may be looked upon by some as what justice and compassion require, but it exacted a huge toll on his family, as well as those close to his family. Robinson had to violate his marriage vows, divorce his wife, and desert his children—all so that he could fool around with his boyfriend. How do his children defend their father to their peers? Is this behavior that the state wants to encourage and uphold as virtuous? Is it good for the families involved, good for the Episcopal communion that Robinson represents, good for society?

Granted, some married, heterosexual men do the same and run off with their girlfriends, which is why the states need to repeal no-fault divorce and hold men (and women) accountable to the promises they make, without any coercion, to their families and to society on their wedding day. But just because no-fault has wreaked havoc on a generation of American children is no excuse for state legislatures to sanction (or for courts to decree) more social pathology with another dubious experiment that, like divorce, treats women and children as disposable.

That not all homosexual debuts are as messy as Robinson's may suggest that women are not always casualties. Nevertheless, being twice as prevalent among males than females, homosexual behavior ends up excluding a portion of women from the sexual equation, not to mention marriage, an injustice that feminists overlook. In other words, homosexuality is mostly about men, who are sexually wrapped up in themselves, directing their passions toward other men who are also wrapped up in themselves.

In 2004 V. Eugene Robinson became the first openly gay man elected as a bishop of the Episcopal Church.

Many critics of gay marriage believe that it does not benefit society.

For the Sake of the Republic

This is not to suggest that gays are self-centered in all aspects of life, as individuals surely make contributions to society that transcend their sexual behavior. But even here, the aggregate contribution of gay couples are muted relative to husband-wife couples. Building upon the insights of Nobel Laureate Gary Becker, who has argued that homosexual couples do not specialize their economic roles as efficiently as do heterosexual couples, economist John Mueller has calculated that average lifetime earnings for married heterosexual couples are significantly higher than all other comparable household arrangements, including a divorced husband and wife in separate households, a cohabiting heterosexual couple, and two same-sex individuals in the same household. The reason: Mueller points to the social science literature that finds, confirming Becker's theory of comparative advantage and the sexual division of labor, that the economic behavior of men changes for the better when they have a wife and children to support, a dynamic missing from same-sex arrangements.

What this comes down to should be obvious: Gay marriage, like all the liberal ideas of the 1970s—including no-fault divorce, abortion on demand, cohabitation, and daycare—does not and cannot serve the common good. When elected officials, like the minister in a wedding ceremony, ask whether the public objects to what is being proposed in Massachusetts and San Francisco, the American people need to rise up and speak their minds for the sake of the children, for the sake of women, and for the sake of the Republic.

EVALUATING THE AUTHORS' ARGUMENTS:

The author of the viewpoint you just read is a conservative scholar whose research focuses on traditional understandings of family and marriage. The author of the following viewpoint is also a scholar but writes his piece from the position of being the parent of a gay child. Does knowing the authors' backgrounds form your opinion of their arguments? If yes, how? Explain your reasoning.

Gay Unions Strengthen Society

Sherman Stein

"Society should encourage such commitments, which not only sustain two people but provide a firm foundation for our society."

In the following viewpoint, Sherman Stein argues that extending marriage to gay couples will help to strengthen society by reinforcing the important values of trust, commitment, and partnership. The author points out that voting, once a right granted only to white males, gradually changed over time as society realized that it was important to include adults of all races and genders in the democratic process. In fact, the author says, gay marriage poses even less of a threat to individuals than enlarging voting rights because gay marriage has no bearing on the relationships straight people have with their spouses or their children. The author concludes that when more people enter into committed and loving relationships, the foundation of society becomes firmer and the world that everyone inhabits becomes a more ideal place.

Sherman Stein is a former mathematics professor at the University of California, Davis.

AS YOU READ, CONSIDER THE FOLLOWING QUESTIONS:
1. What does the author mean when he says, "No one is invading my home or kidnapping my wife or children"?
2. What point is the author trying to make when he mentions the "need for both partners to hold down full-time jobs"?
3. What does the author mean when he uses the word *dilute* to describe the effect of gay unions on marriage?

A quarter of a century ago, our then-teenage daughter, the youngest of our three children, announced that she was gay. Her revelation came as a shock, but the intervening years have given me time to reflect on homosexuality. I have slowly gone from that initial shock to acceptance, along the way reaching some insights.

Committed Couples Strengthen Society

In our world, the word "stranger" calls forth fear. For two people to shift from strangers to friends to devoted lifetime companions is practically

Proponents of gay marriage contend that society should support the union of all committed couples, regardless of their sexual orientation.

Many people believe that heterosexual couples would be altogether unaffected by expanding the definition of marriage to include same-sex unions.

a miracle. Society should encourage such commitments, which not only sustain two people but provide a firm foundation for our society.

All my life I had lived with the idea that "marriage" referred to a man and a woman. Now I wondered, why couldn't the gay world settle for "civil union" with all the legal benefits of marriage. Give us straight people time to adjust to "civil union," then gradually replace that word with "marriage." We need time to absorb new ideas.

I am in the 54th year of a happy marriage. I do not feel that my marriage is threatened by expanding the meaning of the word "marriage." No one is invading my home or kidnapping my wife or children. Nor is the institution of marriage threatened. That people of the same sex might unite in a bond of trust is a far less serious threat to the institution of marriage than the need for both partners to hold down full-time jobs.

Words, Institutions Evolve

Slowly or abruptly, the meanings of words change. Think of the word "vote." Initially, the vote was restricted to men with property. Then

Many gay couples such as this one have challenged state bans on gay marriage in the courts.

it was expanded to include men who had established residency. By the beginning of the Civil War, almost all adult white males could vote. Next, with the passage of the 15th Amendment, blacks, in theory, had the right to vote. Women were granted the vote in 1920. Finally, the vote was extended to everyone 18 years old and over.

There is an underlying similarity between expanding the embrace of the word "vote" and expanding the embrace of the word "marriage." But there is also an important difference. Each time the right to vote was extended, those who already had that right were indeed threatened. They could still vote, but their vote had less impact. But permitting two people of the same sex to form a union graced by the word "marriage" does not jeopardize those already married. It does not dilute the strength of an existing marriage, the way expanding the right to vote diluted the value of existing votes.

A More Compassionate World

I do not understand why some of us are heterosexual and others are homosexual. Why are two of my children heterosexual and one

Expanding the institution of marriage to include gays like this couple could only strengthen society, some say.

homosexual? After decades of research, it is agreed that people do not choose their sexual orientation. I hope that some day we will look upon sexual orientation with the same indifference we give to whether one is right- or left-handed. If we attain that state, we will all be living in a more compassionate world, one with less fear and animosity. Extending the meaning of the word "marriage" will not cause the straight to convert to gay, any more than it would the right-handed person to switch to left-handed.

If we were able to accept the ever-broadening meaning of the vote, which at each stage did threaten the existing order, we can surely absorb the extension of marriage, which will only strengthen the bonds that hold our society together.

EVALUATING THE AUTHORS' ARGUMENTS:

Authors Robert W. Patterson and Sherman Stein disagree on whether including homosexual couples in the institution of marriage would threaten society. However, both authors agree that marriage itself is a key ingredient to a healthy society. In your opinion, is the tradition of marriage instrumental to a strong society? Why or why not?

Gay Couples Threaten the Institution of Marriage

Bernadette Malone

"If male-female isn't a necessary pairing for marriage, why is 'two' a necessary number for marriage?"

Bernadette Malone is the former editorial page editor of the *Union Leader,* a New Hampshire newspaper from which this viewpoint was taken. In the following piece, Malone argues that once the definition of marriage is changed to include people of any gender, there is nothing to stop it from being expanded to include more than two people, or infinite combinations of people, or even incest. Legalizing gay marriage, she warns, would put society on a "slippery slope" down which it will tumble until there is nothing left of the institution of marriage. On these grounds she concludes same-sex marriage must be resisted and marriage must be codified as an institution between a man and a woman.

AS YOU READ, CONSIDER THE FOLLOWING QUESTIONS:

1. According to the author, what is wrong with writer Michael Kinsley's opinion of marriage?

If I were single-handedly responsible for making sure the new Supreme Court ruling overturning state sodomy laws didn't pave the path to gay marriage, as both supporters of the ruling and dissenters predict it will, I'd do a couple of things.

I'd make sure as many people as possible saw pictures from the freaky Gay Pride Parade that culminated in my Greenwich Village neighborhood [in July 2003]. (If straight people celebrated their sexuality with a parade 10 times more licentious than New Orleans' Mardi Gras, I'd oppose heterosexual marriage, too!)

> ## FAST FACT
>
> Approximately fifty thousand to sixty thousand polygamists live in the United States.

I'd make sure as many people as possible knew about the kooky new "queer studies" program at the University of New Hampshire. That'd turn a lot of people off to the idea.

I'd make sure President [George W.] Bush never again referred to marriage between a man and a woman as his "notion"—a word that invites a challenge. One holds a notion that men should open the door for women and no one should wear white after Labor Day. One holds a reasoned conviction that marriage is between one man and one woman.

Gay Marriage Will Open the Door to Polygamy

But the single biggest effort I'd make to stop same-sex marriage is to start pushing for multiple partner marriage. Yep. Polygamy. I'd find some guy out in Utah who ignored the Mormon church's 1830 prohibition against marrying more than one woman. I'd find some wealthy

Muslim residing in the U.S. who wanted to take [the Prophet] Muhammed up on his prescribed allowance of four wives. I'd swallow hard and make common cause with some trashy bigamist from the Jerry Springer Show, and offer to make him an even bigger star by taking his issue all the way to the U.S. Supreme Court. (Forget for a moment that I'm not a lawyer.)

A lesbian couple and their son enjoy a gay pride parade.

Source: Locher. © 2003 by *Chicago Tribune*. Reproduced by permission of Tribune Media Services.

Why would I do that? Because it would force society—more specifically, the five autocratic U.S. Supreme Court justices who have decided to castrate state legislatures and instead rule society themselves—to realize what logically follows from breaking down the definition of marriage. If male-female isn't a necessary pairing for marriage, why is "two" a necessary number for marriage? Why can't three people get married? Or 16, [cult leader] David Koresh–style? As [Supreme Court] Justice Antonin Scalia pointed out in his dissent in [the 2003] *Lawrence v. Texas* case, the Court's decision that the state has no right to regulate sexual behavior between consenting adults means bigamy and all sorts of other behavior (prostitution, incest, etc.) can't be outlawed by states.

Americans Need to Wake Up

I'd be pushing for polygamy to make an ironic point about the desirability of marriage between one man and one woman, the exact formula it takes to create a new child and raise that child with all the benefits of dual-gender influence. That formula, sanctioned by Judeo-

Christian tradition, is supposed to pressure the couple into remaining happily married forever, in large part for their offspring's benefit. I'm all for letting people do what they want in their bedrooms, and I've rolled my eyes when I've lived in states with anti-sodomy laws. But as libertarian as I am, I know the state needs to at least give traditional marriage a nod—if only because children can't be overlooked while adults are out pursuing personal liberty. Otherwise, taxpayers will have to pick up the check for child welfare and therapy bills.

According to the Judeo-Christian tradition and current law, only a married man and woman can properly raise children.

In pushing for polygamy to make my point about gay marriage, I could expect to be joined by the wacky, radical left. Their arguments against traditional marriage, I hope, would wake Americans up. Liberal journalist Michael Kinsley, who you might remember from the early days of CNN's "Crossfire" program, recommends in a *Slate* column that we compromise between gays and straights by refusing to recognize any marriage as legally valid. Let people do whatever they want, in any combination. "And, yes, if three people want to get married, or one person wants to marry herself, and someone else wants to conduct a ceremony and declare them married, let 'em."

And gay activists say same-sex marriage is no threat to traditional marriage!

Gay marriage stands an excellent chance of becoming the law of the land now that the Supreme Court has ruled that states can't "discriminate" against sexual behavior between consenting adults. The best way I can see to get the Supreme Court to rethink that decision is to present it with legalized polygamy—sexual behavior between consenting adults that I think most of us would like to discriminate against.

EVALUATING THE AUTHORS' ARGUMENTS:

In the viewpoint you just read, author Bernadette Malone argues that legalizing same-sex marriage would disastrously threaten the institution of marriage as it now exists. In the following viewpoint, author Tammy Paolino argues that straight couples have already damaged marriage beyond any threat that gay marriage may pose. After reading both viewpoints, which argument do you find more compelling? Why? Explain your answer.

VIEWPOINT 4

Straight Couples Have Already Threatened the Institution of Marriage

Tammy Paolino

"Without any help from those guys on Queer Eye for the Straight Guy, marriage is already in danger of imploding all on its own."

In the following viewpoint, author Tammy Paolino argues that those who claim gay unions will undermine the institution of marriage are in denial about the state of marriage today. She contends that straight couples have already critically threatened marriage, and their hysterical reaction to the suggestion of gay marriage reflects their deep-seated homophobia and confusion about the current state of marriage. In fact, she argues that straight couples have thoroughly disrespected marriage, as evidenced by high rates of divorce, multiple marriages, and high profile cases of infidelity. Furthermore, American culture has celebrated and profited from these debacles, casting doubt on the claim that marriage is a sacred institution that will be besmirched if gay couples are to join it. The author concludes that fears over whether gay marriage will ruin the institution of marriage are misplaced; instead, the straight community must examine how it has damaged marriage and what it can do to restore it.

Columnist Tammy Paolino is features editor at the *Courier-Post* (New Jersey), the newspaper from which this viewpoint was taken.

AS YOU READ, CONSIDER THE FOLLOWING QUESTIONS:
1. What point is the author trying to make by citing Britney Spears' fifty-five-hour marriage?
2. According to the author, what are five social trends that currently threaten marriage?
3. What does the author mean when she writes that arguments she makes in favor of gay marriage are "likely to fall on deaf ears"?

With surprisingly little fanfare, [former New Jersey] Gov. James E. McGreevey on [January 12, 2004] signed the domestic partnership law, extending some health insurance benefits, inheritance and hospital-visitation rights to same-sex couples.

New Jersey joins Massachusetts, Vermont, California and Hawaii in recognizing legal rights of same-sex partners, although, unlike other states, it does not go so far as to sanction gay marriages or civil unions.

Not everyone approves. Among the opponents is the League of American Families, a group that has pledged to challenge the law because it "threatens traditional marriage."

What tradition?

Opponents of Gay Marriage Are Homophobic

Traditional marriage is a fairly modern concept. As much as we would like to believe that, ever since man and woman climbed out of the ooze and began walking upright, they pledged their fidelity and went on to raise happy nuclear families, that is just not the case. You can go back just a few short centuries and find most marriages had more to do with blood lines and financial interests than matters of the heart.

This is not to take anything away from the place marriage has in our society.

Ideally, marriage is a place to grow as a person and find shelter in an often tumultuous world. Folks who share a strong marriage nurture not just each other and their offspring, but everyone else around them. Likewise, a bad marriage often causes pain far beyond the roof beneath which it percolates or disintegrates.

Whatever arguments I might make that you needn't be heterosexual to create a healthy and happy, "'til-death-do-us-part" union are likely to fall on deaf ears. America is clearly divided on the subject of whether marriage is the sacred right of straight couples or the human right of any two people who love each other enough to cast their lot—and their finances—together. Those who oppose the idea of "gay marriage" don't approve of homosexuality at all, and nothing I say here is going to sway them.

Gay rights activists claim that hard statistical evidence discredits the argument that only heterosexual couples create healthy families.

Marriage Faces Many Threats

What I don't understand are those who declare that granting equal legal rights under the law to same-sex couples threatens traditional marriage.

Without any help from those guys on *Queer Eye for the Straight Guy,* marriage is already in danger of imploding all on its own. We know the divorce figures. (I believe it was [actress] Mary Tyler Moore who once expressed amazement at our society's plucky optimism about an institution that fails more than it succeeds.)

Plenty of things do threaten traditional marriage: substance abuse, selfishness, greed, low self-esteem, financial struggles, depression, unre-

A lesbian couple kisses passionately in the midst of an antigay marriage rally. Opponents fear gay marriage would undermine the traditional concept of marriage.

Source: Wright. © 2004 by *Palm Beach Post*. Reproduced by permission of Tribune Media Services.

alistic expectations, domestic abuse, poor role models, the media and its hyper-focus on youth and sex, Internet pornography and chat rooms and more.

Just how sacred do we hold marriage to be, anyway?

Straight Couples Have Dismantled Marriage

After all, ours is a country that elevates reality TV shows, on which people marry for money and power and looks and celebrity, to the top of the ratings.

We've watched our religious leaders tout their marriages as the center of their ministry, only to watch those same marriages come crashing down in an angry storm of tabloid mudslinging. And we've watched a president deny and then, after a fashion, admit to cheating on the First Lady with a young White House intern.

We barely notice when Hollywood celebrities—who, after all, are as close as you get to American royalty—marry five, six, seven times.

And if our own marriages bare little resemblance to the romantic adventures of [Elizabeth Taylor] or Liza [Minnelli], we nonetheless aren't all that shocked when a friend or relative calls it quits after decades of marriage.

Recent water cooler gabfests have been abuzz with the news that Britney Spears and a friend had gotten hitched and then unhitched. Their "marriage" lasted 55 hours.

Before we begin blaming committed gay couples for dismantling the institution of marriage, maybe we should look around and take stock of what we ourselves are doing to protect it in the first place.

EVALUATING THE AUTHOR'S ARGUMENTS:

In the viewpoint you just read, author Tammy Paolino suggests that homophobia, or contempt for gay people, explains why many people oppose gay marriage. Considering what you have read on the subject, what role do you believe homophobia plays in the gay marriage debate? Is it possible to be against gay marriage but not homophobic? Explain your answer.

Gay Marriage Would Threaten Children

Maggie Gallagher

"All kids need and deserve a married mom and dad."

In the following viewpoint, author Maggie Gallagher argues that gay marriage should be banned because it presents a dangerous alternative to the family structure, which will impede the development of children. She contends that the overwhelming purpose of marriage is to provide a safe, nurturing, instructional environment for children. This environment can only consist of two parents, one of each gender, who are in a committed relationship. But gay couples cannot provide a parent from each gender, and the author argues that children raised in this environment will suffer from abnormal development. If same-sex couples choose to raise children, the author charges they are guilty of elevating their own sexual desires over the needs of children. The author concludes that a society that encourages people to satisfy their sexual needs over rearing healthy children is socially irresponsible and in grave danger.

Maggie Gallagher, president of the Institute for Marriage and Public Policy, has written extensively on issues of marriage and family in America. Her articles have appeared in the *National Review* and the *Weekly Standard,* from which this viewpoint is taken.

AS YOU READ, CONSIDER THE FOLLOWING QUESTIONS:
1. In the viewpoint you just read, why does the author refer to Greek, Roman, Jewish, and Christian culture?
2. What does the author mean when she describes some children as "throwaway kids"?
3. What point do you think the author is trying to make when she discusses her findings that only one one-hundredth of 1 percent of General Motors employees opted to cover their partner under their health benefits?

Gay marriage is no longer a theoretical issue. Canada has it. Massachusetts is expected to get it any day. The Goodridge decision there could set off a legal, political, and cultural battle in the courts of 50 states and in the U.S. Congress. Every politician, every judge, every citizen has to decide: Does same-sex marriage matter? If so, how and why? . . .

Marriage Is for Socializing Children

Marriage is the fundamental, cross-cultural institution for bridging the male-female divide so that children have loving, committed mothers and fathers. Marriage is inherently normative: It is about holding out a certain kind of relationship as a social ideal, especially when there are children involved. Marriage is not simply an artifact of law; neither is it a mere delivery mechanism for a set of legal benefits that might as well be shared more broadly. The laws of marriage do not create marriage, but in societies ruled by law they help trace the boundaries and sustain the public meanings of marriage.

In other words, while individuals freely choose to enter marriage, society upholds the marriage option, formalizes its definition, and surrounds it with norms and reinforcements, so we can raise boys and girls who aspire to become the kind of men and women who can make successful marriages. Without this shared, public aspect, perpetuated generation after generation, marriage becomes what its critics say it is: a mere contract, a vessel with no particular content, one of a menu of sexual lifestyles, of no fundamental importance to anyone outside a given relationship.

The marriage idea is that children need mothers and fathers, that societies need babies, and that adults have an obligation to shape their sexual behavior so as to give their children stable families in which to grow up. . . .

Mothers and Fathers Are Needed

Marriage is a virtually universal human institution. In all the wildly rich and various cultures flung throughout the ecosphere, in society after society, whether tribal or complex, and however bizarre, human beings have created systems of publicly approved sexual union between men and women that entail well-defined responsibilities of mothers and fathers. Not all these marriage systems look like our own, which is rooted in a fusion of Greek, Roman, Jewish, and Christian culture. Yet everywhere, in isolated mountain valleys, parched deserts, jungle thickets, and broad plains, people have come up with some version of this thing called marriage. Why?

Marriage is an almost universal institution, and notions of its sanctity are usually passed down from generation to generation.

Because sex between men and women makes babies, that's why. Even today, in our technologically advanced contraceptive culture, half of all pregnancies are unintended: Sex between men and women *still* makes babies. Most men and women are powerfully drawn to perform a sexual act that can and does generate life. Marriage is our attempt to reconcile and harmonize the erotic, social, sexual, and financial needs of men and women with the needs of their partner and their children.

How to reconcile the needs of children with the sexual desires of adults? Every society has to face that question, and some resolve it in ways that

Loving couples often choose to marry in order to provide a stable family environment for any children they might have.

inflict horrendous cruelty on children born outside marriage. Some cultures decide these children don't matter: Men can have all the sex they want, and any children they create outside of marriage will be throwaway kids; marriage is for citizens—slaves and peasants need not apply.[1]. . .

Our better tradition, and the only one consistent with democratic principles, is to hold up a single ideal for all parents, which is ultimately based on our deep cultural commitment to the equal dignity and social worth of all children. All kids need and deserve a married mom and dad. All parents are supposed to at least try to behave in ways that will give their own children this important protection. Privately, religiously, emotionally, individually, marriage may have many meanings. But this is the core of its public, shared meaning: Marriage is the place where having children is not only tolerated but welcomed and encouraged, because it gives children mothers and fathers. . . .

Gay Marriage Encourages Dysfunctional Families

The problem with endorsing gay marriage is not that it would allow a handful of people to choose alternative family forms, but that it would require society at large to gut marriage of its central presumptions about family in order to accommodate a few adults' desires. . . .

Same-sex marriage would enshrine in law a public judgment that the desire of adults for families of choice outweighs the need of children for mothers and fathers. It would give sanction and approval to the creation of a motherless or fatherless family as a deliberately chosen "good." It would mean the law was neutral as to whether children had mothers and fathers. Motherless and fatherless families would be deemed just fine. . . .

It is also true, as gay-marriage advocates note, that we impose no fertility tests for marriage: Infertile and older couples marry, and not every fertile couple chooses procreation. But every marriage between a man

1. Historically, in some cultures slaves and peasants have been prohibited from marrying.

In the view of those who reason that healthy children need one parent of each gender, these lesbians make altogether unfit parents to their adopted daughter.

and a woman is capable of giving any child they create or adopt a mother and a father. Every marriage between a man and a woman discourages either from creating fatherless children outside the marriage vow. In this sense, neither older married couples nor childless husbands and wives publicly challenge or dilute the core meaning of marriage. Even when a man marries an older woman and they do not adopt, his marriage helps protect children. How? His marriage means, if he keeps his vows, that he will not produce out-of-wedlock children.

Marriage Requires a Husband and a Wife

Does marriage discriminate against gays and lesbians? Formally speaking, no. There are no sexual-orientation tests for marriage; many gays and lesbians do choose to marry members of the opposite sex, and some of these unions succeed. Our laws do not require a person to marry the individual to whom he or she is most erotically attracted, so long as he or she is willing to promise sexual fidelity, mutual caretaking, and shared parenting of any children of the marriage.

But marriage is unsuited to the wants and desires of many gays and lesbians, precisely because it is designed to bridge the male-female divide and sustain the idea that children need mothers and fathers. To make a marriage, what you need is a husband and a wife. Redefining marriage so that it suits gays and lesbians would require fundamentally changing our legal, public, and social conception of what marriage is in ways that threaten its core public purposes. . . .

Morally Callous and Socially Irresponsible

Meanwhile, *cui bono* [who benefits]? To meet the desires of whom would we put our most basic social institution at risk? No good research on the marriage intentions of homosexual people exists. For what it's worth, the Census Bureau reports that 0.5 percent of households now consist of same-sex partners. To get a proxy for how many gay couples would avail themselves of the health insurance benefits marriage can provide [if gay marriage were to be legalized], I asked the top 10 companies listed on the Human Rights Campaign's website as providing same-sex insurance benefits how many of their employees use this option. Only one company, General Motors, released its data. Out of 1.3 million employees, 166 claimed benefits for a same-sex partner, *one one-hundredth of one percent.*

People who argue for creating gay marriage do so in the name of high ideals: justice, compassion, fairness. Their sincerity is not in question. Nevertheless, to take the already troubled institution most responsible for the protection of children and throw out its most basic presumption in order to further adult interests in sexual freedom would not be high-minded. It would be morally callous and socially irresponsible.

EVALUATING THE AUTHORS' ARGUMENTS:

In the viewpoint you just read, author Maggie Gallagher believes that children need two heterosexual parents, one of each gender, in order to be properly raised. In the following viewpoint, author E.J. Graff believes that children can be raised just as well by gay parents. After reading both viewpoints, do you think that it is better for children to be raised by opposite-sex couples or by same-sex couples, or is there little difference? Use evidence from the viewpoints to support your argument.

VIEWPOINT 6

Gay Marriage Would Nurture Children

E.J. Graff

In the following viewpoint, E.J. Graff argues that gay and lesbian parents are capable of raising healthy, happy children. What is most important, argues the author, is that children are raised in a loving home by committed and content parents. Graff argues that it is unfair to expect gay parents to do better than their heterosexual counterparts. She concludes that granting gay couples the right to marry and raise children will provide more stable two-parent homes that will serve to nurture children and in turn benefit society.

E.J. Graff is a contributing editor at the *American Prospect,* from which this viewpoint was taken. She is also the author of *What Is Marriage For? The Strange Social History of Our Most Intimate Institution.*

"Children of lesbian or gay parents turn out just fine."

AS YOU READ, CONSIDER THE FOLLOWING QUESTIONS:

1. According to the author, how many studies have been done on the children of lesbians and gay men?
2. Are the children of gay and lesbian parents more likely to become homosexual, according to the author?
3. What was the conclusion of the February 2002 American Academy of Pediatrics report?

E.J. Graff, "The Other Marriage War: There's One Group That Is Pursuing Legal Union, and Its Kids Need the Stability," *The American Prospect,* vol. 13, April 8, 2002. Copyright © 2002 by The American Prospect, Inc., 11 Beacon St., Suite 1120, Boston, MA 02108. All rights reserved. Reproduced by permission.

Welcome to the world of lesbian and gay parents, where you can be a parent one day and not the next; in one state but not another; when you're straight but not when you're gay. At any moment, your heterosexual ex might find a judge willing to yank the kids after you come out. Or you might hear your parental fitness debated by strangers—on radio, on TV, and in newspapers—using language that makes your children wake up at night from dreams that the government has taken you away.

Yes, the climate for lesbian and gay parents has improved dramatically in the past 20 years. . . . The lesbian baby boom began in Boston and San Francisco in the mid-1980s. In both cities, after mainstream

A lesbian couple in Boston applies for a marriage license. Extending marriage rights to gay couples would provide stable two-parent homes to countless adoptable children.

doctors refused to offer donor insemination (DI) services to unmarried women, lesbians started their own sperm banks and DI clinics. Since then, two-mom families have popped up everywhere from Maine to Utah, from Alaska to Florida. In smaller numbers, gay dads have followed, taking in foster children, hiring surrogates, or adopting (as individuals, if necessary) whenever they could find birth moms, local authorities, or judges who'd help. And that's only the latest incarnation of gay and lesbian parenting. Lesbians and gay men have long become parents the conventional way: through heterosexual marriage.

The number of gay-parent households has steadily increased since the mid-1980s.

But law is lagging badly behind this social transformation. Although many . . . readers may know two-mom or two-dad families, they probably do not know about the daily legal insecurity, the extra level of anxiety and effort, and the occasional shocking injustices those families face. Society is still profoundly ambivalent about lesbians and gay men—and about the unfamiliar, sometimes queasy-making idea of queers raising kids. As a result, unpredictable legal decisions about lesbian and gay parents too often leave their children in limbo.

The Kids Are All Right

Is there any reason to worry about how these kids are raised? No. More than 20 studies have been done on about 300 children of lesbians and gay men. Some compare children of divorced lesbian moms or gay dads with children of divorced heterosexual moms or dads; others compare two-mom families with mom-and-pop families that used the same DI clinic. The results are quite clear: Children of lesbian or gay parents turn out just fine on every conceivable measure of emotional and social development: attachment, self-esteem, moral judgment, behavior, intelligence, likability, popularity, gender identity, family warmth, and all sorts of obscure psychological concepts. Whatever the scale, children with lesbian or gay parents and children with heterosexual parents turn out equally well—and grow up to be heterosexual in the same overwhelming proportions. . . .

That's why organizations such as the American Psychological Association, the National Association of Social Workers, the American Academy of Child and Adolescent Psychiatry, and the American Counseling Association have released statements in support of lesbian and gay parents. In February [2002], for instance, the American

> ## FAST FACT
>
> In 1995 the American Psychological Association found that children raised by gay parents are not disadvantaged in any significant way compared to the children of heterosexual parents. Three subsequent studies by other organizations, such as the American Academy of Child and Adolescent Psychiatry and the American Academy of Pediatrics, confirmed these results.

Academy of Pediatrics came out with a report that had been vetted by an unprecedented number of committees and had taken four years to wend its way toward the academy's full approval. Its conclusion: "No data have pointed to any risk to children as a result of growing up in a family with one or more gay parents." Nor, the AAP found, is parents' sexual orientation an important variable in how kids turn out.

So what is? If basics like food, shelter, clothing, and health care are covered, what matters to kids is the happiness and satisfaction of the parents. Are the parents happily mated and content with the way household responsibilities are shared? Or are they miserable and sniping at each other, whether together or separated? You can guess which type of household will produce happier and more confident kids. Harmony helps children; conflict and disruption hurt. Despite the yammering of the conservative marriage movement, how households are run matters more than who (read: which sex or sexual orientation) runs them. . . .

Providing a stable and nurturing environment is an important part of raising children, regardless of the sexual orientation of the parents.

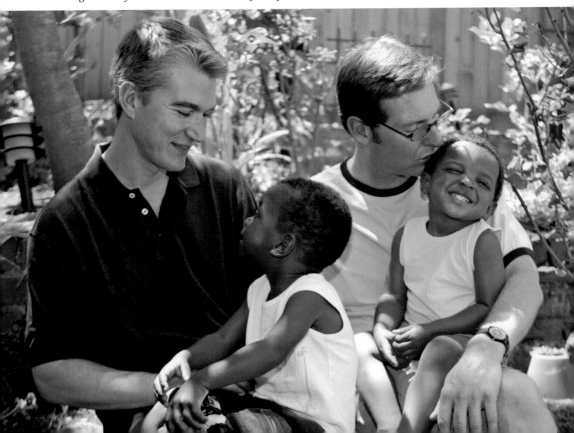

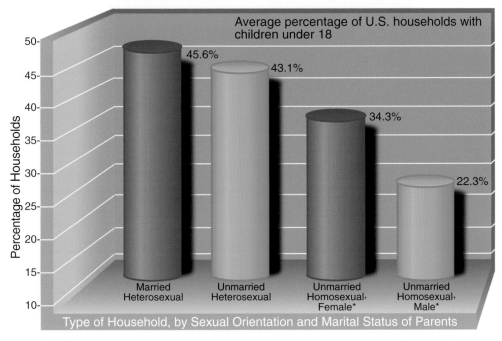

Many Gay Couples Have Children

Average percentage of U.S. households with children under 18

Percentage of Households

45.6%
43.1%
34.3%
22.3%

Married Heterosexual | Unmarried Heterosexual | Unmarried Homosexual, Female* | Unmarried Homosexual, Male*

Type of Household, by Sexual Orientation and Marital Status of Parents

*The children either belong to one of the partners or are biologically unrelated, such as foster children or adoptees.
Source: "Married-Couple and Unmarried-Partner Households: 2000," U.S. Census Bureau, 2000.

Gay Parents Need Marriage Rights

So what do these children need from society? The same thing all children need: clear and enforceable ties to their parents. Child psychologist Anna Freud once wrote that children "can handle almost anything better than instability." Not coincidentally, trying to shore up a family's stability is the goal of much marriage-and-family law. . . .

So what, besides social tolerance, should the forces of good be working for? Policies and laws that tie these kids firmly to their real, daily parents. These children need strong statutes that let co-moms and co-dads adopt—preferably without the intrusive home study, the thousands of dollars in legal fees, and the reference letters from colleagues and friends that are now required. They need decisive guidelines saying that an adoption in one state is an adoption in every state. And they need marriage rights for their parents. Much of marriage law is designed to help spouses rear families, letting them make a single shelter from their combined incomes, assets, benefits, pensions, habits, strengths, weaknesses, and knowledge. Today, when a heterosexual married couple uses DI, the man is automatically the legal father (as long as he has consented in writing) without having to adopt; if any marriage (or even some lesser system of recognition, like civil unions or registered partnership) were possible, the same could and should be true for lesbians.

By taking up this banner, liberals and progressives can prove that they have a practical commitment to real families and real children. As an Ontario judge wrote in 1995: "When one reflects on the seemingly limitless parade of neglected, abandoned and abused children who appear before our courts in protection cases daily, all of whom have been in the care of heterosexual parents in a 'traditional' family structure, the suggestion that it might not ever be in the best interests of these children to be raised by loving, caring, and committed parents who might happen to be lesbian or gay, is nothing short of ludicrous."

EVALUATING THE AUTHOR'S ARGUMENTS:

In the viewpoint you just read, E.J. Graff argues that family instability, such as divorce, is the most detrimental thing to a child's development, and therefore as long as gay couples are stable they will raise healthy children. Critics of gay parenting argue that even divorced families, because they consist of a mother and a father, provide a better atmosphere for children to be raised in. What is your opinion on this issue?

GLOSSARY

antimiscegenation laws: Laws that prohibited people of different races from marrying. The country's last antimiscegenation laws were struck down in 1967 in a Supreme Court case known as *Loving v. Virginia.*

civil disobedience: A form of typically nonviolent protest in which protestors deliberately violate or refuse to obey a law in order to draw attention to its unfairness. The main purpose of civil disobedience is to challenge a prevailing status quo. During the 1960s' civil rights movement, for example, acts of civil disobedience included boycotting racist bus lines and crossing segregated public spaces. In 2004, the act of handing out marriage licenses to gay couples in San Francisco was considered by many to be a form of civil disobedience.

civil rights movement: An American social movement during the 1950s and 1960s that was led primarily by African Americans in an effort to establish the civil rights of black citizens. It resulted in legislation that federally prohibited discrimination on the basis of skin color, race, religion, or ethnicity. It also led to the desegregation of public schools, parks, clubs, and other establishments.

Defense of Marriage Act (DOMA): A federal law enacted in September 1996 that states the federal government will only recognize marriage as an institution between one man and one woman. However, DOMA also allows each state in the union to recognize or deny relationships between persons of the same sex as it sees fit.

federalism: A system of government in which power is divided between a central authority and individual units, such as states. Advocates of federalism believe that states should have the authority to make most decisions for themselves, instead of power being centrally concentrated in the hands of the federal government.

Federal Marriage Amendment: A proposed amendment to the U.S. Constitution that would define marriage as a union between a man and a woman and would ban gay marriage in the United States. Such an amendment would prevent states from recognizing same-sex marriages, as Massachusetts chose to do in 2003. Adopting a Federal Marriage Amendment is a high priority of the Bush administration.

Goodridge decision (*Goodridge v. Department of Public Health*): The November 2003 Massachusetts Supreme Court decision that legalized gay marriage in that state. In the case, it was decided that excluding gay couples from marriage, but allowing them "civil union" partnerships, constituted an unconstitutional "separate but equal" situation. Thus, to ensure equality, gay couples were granted the right to marry by the court. The controversial ruling is set to be reviewed in 2006 and could be repealed by state or federal action.

Lawrence v. Texas: A 2003 case in which the U.S. Supreme Court invalidated Texas laws which prohibited sex between two men. The court decided that intimate consensual sexual conduct was part of the liberty that is protected under the Fourteenth Amendment, and thus declared Texas's antisodomy laws unconstitutional.

no-fault divorce: A type of divorce that may be granted without showing that either spouse was guilty of some form of marital misconduct, such as infidelity or abuse. No-fault divorce allows the couple to split simply if one of them is unhappy in the marriage.

polygamy: The practice of having multiple wives. Also known as bigamy.

transgender: A person who appears as or wishes to be considered a member of their opposite sex. Transgendered people often undergo surgery to biologically change their sex.

FACTS ABOUT GAY MARRIAGE

Gay Marriage Around the World
- The Netherlands became the first country in the world to legalize same-sex marriages on April 1, 2001.
- According to United Press International, less than 10 percent of the fifty thousand estimated same-sex couples in the Netherlands have opted to marry.
- Denmark, Sweden, Norway, Finland, and Iceland grant same-sex couples the same rights as heterosexual couples.
- Argentina, Canada, Hungary, France, Portugal, Britain, and Germany grant some form of civil unions to same-sex couples.
- South Africa has recognized gay rights in its constitution since 1994, and activists are lobbying to have same-sex couples included in common law marriage legislation, as is the situation in Portugal.
- Belgium legalized gay marriage in 2002.
- Italy and Spain are two of the many countries around the world that do not legally recognize same-sex relationships.
- Some Swiss cities, such as Zurich and Geneva, provide certain legal rights to same-sex couples.

According to the International Gay & Lesbian Human Rights Commission:
- Homosexual acts are illegal in many countries, including Afghanistan, Algeria, Barbados, Botswana, Cameroon, Ethiopia, Georgia, India, Iran, Kenya, Malaysia, Morocco, Nepal, Nicaragua, Sri Lanka, Syria, and Zimbabwe.
- In Botswana, sex between two men is punishable with up to seven years in prison, while in India, perpetrators can be sentenced to up to life in prison. In Iran, those found guilty of homosexuality can be put to death in one of four ways: being hanged, stoned, halved by a sword, or dropped from the highest perch.

Gay Marriage in the United States
- Over forty-two hundred same-sex couples have received marriage licenses since May 17, 2004, when Massachusetts first began issuing them to gay couples.

- In February 2004, San Francisco mayor Gavin Newsom began issuing marriage licenses to same-sex couples in that city. Gay couples traveled from all around the country to obtain a legal marriage license, even if it would not be recognized by their home state.
- Nearly four thousand same-sex couples obtained marriage licenses in San Francisco in the four weeks before the California state Supreme Court halted the process. In August 2004, the court invalidated the licenses, declaring that Mayor Newsom had overstepped his authority in issuing them.
- Vermont has granted civil union status for gay couples since 2000. It is the only state in America to do so.
- Just ten states specifically allow gay and lesbian couples to adopt kids: California, Connecticut, Illinois, New Jersey, New York, Pennsylvania, Massachusetts, Vermont, Washington, and Wisconsin.
- There are approximately 10 million children in the United States who have at least one parent who is gay or lesbian.
- Demographers expect the prospect of gay marriage to become more popular as the American public gets older. According to the *Economist,* just 21 percent of those over 65 support gay marriage, while 55 percent of 18- to 29-year-olds do.

Homosexuality in the United States

- It is difficult to say exactly how many homosexuals live in the United States because many gay or lesbian people may not be "out" about their sexual identity. Estimates range from between 1 and 10 percent of the total population that is homosexual.
- It is most often estimated that about 2.8 percent of all American men are gay, while 1.4 percent of all American women are lesbian. Interestingly, according to a September 2002 Gallup poll, the American public thinks that 21.4 percent of all men are gay and 22 percent of all women are lesbians.
- On the 2000 Census, 594,391 American households identified themselves as same-sex unmarried partners, representing 1.2 million gay and lesbian adults.

National Surveys About Gay Marriage

According to a Quinnipiac University poll taken in December 2004:

- Although 65 percent of those surveyed said they do not think same-sex marriage should be legalized, 53 percent of those surveyed said they opposed amending the U.S. Constitution to ban same-sex marriage.

- Forty-five percent of those surveyed would support the right of same-sex couples to form civil unions.

According to a November 2004 poll conducted jointly by CBS News and the *New York Times:*

- Thirty-one percent of Democrats surveyed said they thought same-sex marriage should be legalized, while just 9 percent of Republicans did.
- When asked their views on whether same-sex couples should have civil union rights instead of the right to marry, 36 percent of Republicans surveyed supported this arrangement, while 30 percent of Democrats did.
- Fifty-four percent of Republicans surveyed thought there should be no legal recognition of same-sex relationships; 54 percent of Democrats surveyed agreed.

According to a Harris poll taken in April 2004:

- Twenty-seven percent of Americans surveyed said they supported the right of same-sex couples to marry. But when asked how they would feel about gay marriage if their son or daughter were gay, 36 percent of Americans said they would support legalizing gay marriage.
- Forty percent of Americans surveyed said they believed the federal government should make decisions about gay marriage, while 41 percent said they believed the states should rule individually on gay marriage.

ORGANIZATIONS TO CONTACT

The editors have compiled the following list of organizations concerned with the issues debated in this book. The descriptions are derived from materials provided by the organizations. All have publications or information available for interested readers. The list was compiled on the date of publication of the present volume; the information provided here may change. Be aware that many organizations take several weeks or longer to respond to inquiries, so allow as much time as possible.

American Civil Liberties Union (ACLU)
132 W. Forty-third St., New York, NY 10036
(212) 944-9800
fax: (212) 359-5290
Web site: www.aclu.org

The ACLU is the nation's oldest and largest civil liberties organization. Its Lesbian and Gay Rights/AIDS Project, started in 1986, handles litigation, education, and public policy work on behalf of gays and lesbians. The ACLU publishes the handbook *The Rights of Lesbians and Gay Men,* the briefing paper "Lesbian and Gay Rights," and the monthly newsletter *Civil Liberties Alert.*

American Family Communiversity (AFCO)
511 N. Oakley Blvd., Chicago, IL 60612
(312) 738-2275
fax: (312) 738-2207

AFCO is a multidisciplinary action and education agency engaged in upgrading the various policies, practices, procedures, professions, systems, and institutions affecting the stability and viability of marriage. It publishes the books *Divorce for the Unbroken Marriage* and *Therapeutic Family Law* as well as several monographs.

Canadian Lesbian and Gay Archives (CLGA)
Box 639, Station A, Toronto, ON M5W 1G2 Canada
(416) 777-2755
Web site: www.clga.ca/archives

The CLGA collects and maintains information and materials relating to the gay and lesbian rights movement in Canada and elsewhere. Its collection of records and other materials documenting the stories of lesbians and gay men and their organizations in Canada is available to the public for the purpose of education and research. It also publishes an annual newsletter, *Lesbian and Gay Archivist.*

Children of Lesbians and Gays Everywhere (COLAGE)
3543 Eighteenth St., Suite 1, San Francisco, CA 94110
(415) 861-5437
fax: (415) 255-8345
e-mail: colage@colage.org
Web site: www.colage.org

COLAGE is a national and international organization that supports young people with lesbian, gay, bisexual, and transgender (LGBT) parents. Their mission is to foster the growth of daughters and sons of LGBT parents by providing education, support, and community. Their publications include such newsletters as *Tips for Making Classrooms Safer for Students with LGBT Parents* and *COLAGE Summary.*

Concerned Women for America (CWFA)
1015 Fifteenth St. NW, Suite 1100, Washington, DC 20005
(202) 488-7000
fax: (202) 488-0806
e-mail: mail@cwfa.org
Web site: www.cwfa.org

The CWFA is an educational and legal defense foundation that seeks to strengthen the traditional family by promoting Judeo-Christian moral standards. It opposes gay marriage and the granting of additional civil rights protections to gays and lesbians. The CWFA publishes the monthly magazine *Family Voice* and various position papers on gay marriage and other issues.

Courage
c/o Church of St. John the Baptist, 210 W. Thirty-first St.,
New York, NY 10001
(212) 268-1010
fax: (212) 268-7150

e-mail: NYCourage@aol.com
Web site: http://CourageRC.net

Courage is a network of spiritual support groups for gay and lesbian Catholics who wish to lead celibate lives in accordance with Roman Catholic teachings on homosexuality. It publishes listings of local groups, a newsletter, and an annotated bibliography of books on homosexuality.

Equal Rights Marriage Fund (ERMF)
2001 M St. NW, Washington, DC 20036
(202) 822-6546
fax: (202) 466-3540

The ERMF is dedicated to the legalization of gay and lesbian marriage and serves as a national clearinghouse for information on same-sex marriage. The organization publishes several brochures and articles, including *Gay Marriage: A Civil Right.*

Family Research Council (FRC)
700 Thirteenth St. NW, Suite 500, Washington, DC 20005
(202) 393-2100
fax: (202) 393-2134

The council is a research, resource, and educational organization that promotes the traditional family, which the council defines as a group of people bound by marriage, blood, or adoption. The council opposes gay marriage and adoption rights. It publishes numerous reports from a conservative perspective on issues affecting the family, including homosexuality. These publications include the monthly newsletter *Washington Watch* and bimonthly journal *Family Policy.*

Family Research Institute (FRI)
PO Box 62640, Colorado Springs, CO 80962-0640
(303) 681-3113
Web site: www.familyresearchinst.org

The FRI distributes information about family, sexuality, and substance abuse issues. It believes that strengthening marriage would reduce many social problems, including crime, poverty, and sexually transmitted diseases. The institute publishes the bimonthly newsletter *Family Research Report* as well as the position paper "What's Wrong with Gay Marriage?"

Focus on the Family

8605 Explorer Dr., Colorado Springs, CO 80920

(800) 232-6459

fax: (719) 548-4525

Web site: www.family.org

Focus on the Family is a conservative Christian organization that promotes traditional family values and gender roles. Its publications include the monthly magazine *Focus on the Family* and the reports *Setting the Record Straight: What Research Really Says About the Social Consequences of Homosexuality, No-Fault Fallout: The Grim Aftermath of Modern Divorce Law and How to Change It, Only a Piece of Paper? The Unquestionable Benefits of Lifelong Marriage,* and *"Only a Piece of Paper?" The Social Significance of the Marriage License and the Negative Consequences of Cohabitation.*

Howard Center for Family, Religion, and Society

934 N. Main St., Rockford, IL 61103

(815) 964-5819

fax: (815) 965-1826

Web site: www.profam.org

The purpose of the Howard Center is to provide research and understanding that demonstrates and affirms family and religion as the foundation of a virtuous and free society. The center believes that the natural family is the fundamental unit of society. The primary mission of the Howard Center is to provide a clearinghouse of useful and relevant information to support families and their defenders throughout the world. The center publishes the monthly journal, *Family in America,* and the *Religion and Society Report.*

Human Rights Campaign (HRC)

919 Eighteenth St. NW, Suite 800, Washington, DC 20006

(202) 628-4160

fax: (202) 347-5323

Web site: www.hrc.org

The HRC provides information on national political issues affecting lesbian, gay, bisexual, and transgender Americans. It offers resources to educate congressional leaders and the public on critical issues such as ending workplace discrimination, combating hate crimes, fighting HIV/AIDS, protecting gay and lesbian families, and working for better lesbian health. HRC publishes the *HRC Quarterly* and *LAWbriefs.*

IntiNet Resource Center
PO Box 4322, San Rafael, CA 94913
e-mail: pad@well.com

The center promotes nonmonogamous relationships as an alternative to the traditional family. It also serves as a clearinghouse for information on nonmonogamous relationships and as a network for people interested in alternative family lifestyles. IntiNet publishes the quarterly newsletter *Floodtide,* the book *Polyamory: The New Love Without Limits,* and the *Resource Guide for the Responsible Non-Monogamist.*

Lambda Legal Defense and Education Fund, Inc.
666 Broadway, Suite 1200, New York, NY 10012
(212) 995-8585
fax: (212) 995-2306

Lambda is a public-interest law firm committed to achieving full recognition of the civil rights of lesbians, gay men, and people with HIV/AIDS. The firm addresses a variety of areas, including equal marriage rights, the military, parenting and relationship issues, and domestic-partner benefits. It publishes the quarterly *Lambda Update* and the pamphlet *Freedom to Marry.*

Loving More
PO Box 4358, Boulder, CO 80306
(303) 534-7540
e-mail: ryan@lovemore.com.
Web site: www.lovemore.com

Loving More explores and supports many different forms of family and relationships. It promotes alternative relationship options—such as open marriage, extended family, and multipartner marriages—and serves as a national clearinghouse for the multipartner movement. The organization publishes the quarterly magazine *Loving More.*

National Center for Lesbian Rights
870 Market St., Suite 570, San Francisco, CA 94102
(415) 392-6257
fax: (415) 392-8442

The center is a public-interest law office providing legal counseling and representation for victims of sexual-orientation discrimination. Primary areas of advice include child custody and parenting, employment, housing, the military, and insurance. Among the center's publications are the handbooks *Recognizing Lesbian and Gay Families: Strategies for Obtaining Domestic Partners Benefits* and *Lesbian and Gay Parenting: A Psychological and Legal Perspective.*

National Gay and Lesbian Task Force (NGLTF)
2320 Seventeenth St. NW, Washington, DC 20009-2702
(202) 332-6483
fax: (202) 332-0207

NGLTF is a civil-rights advocacy organization that lobbies Congress and the White House on a range of civil rights and AIDS issues. The organization is working to make same-sex marriage legal. It publishes numerous papers and pamphlets, and the booklet *To Have and to Hold: Organizing for Our Right to Marry* and the fact sheet "Lesbian and Gay Families."

The Rockford Institute Center on the Family in America
934 N. Main St., Rockford, IL 61103
(815) 964-5811
fax: (815) 965-1826

The Rockford Institute works to return America to Judeo-Christian values and supports traditional roles for men and women. Its Center on the Family in America studies the evolution of the family and the effects of divorce on society. The institute publishes the monthly periodical *Chronicles* and the newsletter *Main Street Memorandum.*

Traditional Values Coalition
139 C St. SE, Washington, DC 20003
(202) 547-8570
fax: (202) 546-6403

The coalition strives to restore what the group believes are traditional moral and spiritual values in American government, schools, media, and the fiber of American society. It believes that gay rights threaten the family unit and extend civil rights beyond what the coalition considers appropriate limits. The coalition publishes the quarterly newsletter *Traditional Values Report,* as well as various information papers, one of which specifically addresses same-sex marriage.

Books

Tammy Bruce, *The Death of Right and Wrong: Exposing the Left's Assault on Our Culture and Values.* Roseville, CA: Forum/Prima, 2003. The author argues that political issues such as gay marriage have led America to become a moral vacuum that no longer distinguishes between right and wrong.

Kate Burns, *At Issue: Gay and Lesbian Families.* San Diego: Greenhaven Press, 2005. This short anthology offers various viewpoints on homosexual families. Excellent for young readers.

Sean Cahill, *Same-Sex Marriage in the United States: Focus on the Facts.* Lanham, MD: Lexington Books, 2004. This book, written by the director of the Policy Institute of the National Gay and Lesbian Task Force, uses statistical information to explore both the pro- and antigay marriage movements.

George Chauncey, *Why Marriage? The History Shaping Today's Debate over Gay Equality.* Cambridge, MA: Basic Books, 2004. A primer on the history of the gay rights debate in the United States.

James Dobson, *Marriage Under Fire: Why We Must Win This Battle.* Sisters, OR: Multnomah, 2004. This antigay marriage book argues that the gay movement seeks to undermine the American family.

Jane Drucker, *Lesbian and Gay Families Speak Out: Understanding the Joys and Challenges of Diverse Family Life.* Reading, MA: Perseus, 2001. This anecdotal book draws on the experiences of real families to argue that children can thrive when raised by homosexual parents.

William N. Eskridge, *The Case for Same-Sex Marriage: From Sexual Liberty to Civilized Commitment.* New York: Free Press, 1996. This pro-gay marriage book argues that America should legalize same-sex marriage because more marriage will enhance civilization.

Ronnie W. Floyd, *The Gay Agenda: It's Dividing the Family, the Church, and a Nation.* Green Forest, AR: New Leaf Press, 2004. A religious argument against same-sex marriage.

Abigail Garner, *Families Like Mine: Children of Gay Parents Tell It Like It Is.* New York: HarperCollins, 2004. Personal accounts of growing up in nontraditional families. Good for young adult readers.

Evan Gerstmann, *Same-Sex Marriage and the Constitution.* New York: Cambridge University Press, 2004. Explores the legal and constitutional ramifications of the gay marriage debate.

E.J. Graff, *What Is Marriage For? The Strange Social History of Our Most Intimate Institution.* Boston: Beacon Press, 1999. Explores the meaning of marriage around the world throughout history.

Noelle Howey et al., *Out of the Ordinary: Essays on Growing Up with Gay, Lesbian, and Transgender Parents.* New York: Stonewall Inn Editions, 2000. The personal experiences of children raised in gay households.

Davina Kotulski, *Why You Should Give a Damn About Gay Marriage.* Los Angeles: Advocate Books, 2004. This pro-gay marriage book focuses on the rights, benefits, and privileges extended to married couples.

Erwin W. Lutzer, *The Truth About Same-Sex Marriage: Six Things You Need to Know About What's Really at Stake.* Chicago: Moody, 2004. A Christian argument against gay marriage.

David Moats, *Civil Wars: A Battle for Gay Marriage.* Orlando: Harcourt, 2004. Written by a Pulitzer Prize–winning journalist, this book chronicles the struggle over marriage since 2000.

Jonathan Rauch, *Gay Marriage: Why It Is Good for Gays, Good for Straights, and Good for America.* New York: Times Books–Henry Holt, 2004. A leading Washington journalist argues that gay marriage is the best way to preserve and protect society's most essential institution.

Alan Sears and Craig Osten, *The Homosexual Agenda: Exposing the Principal Threat to Religious Freedom Today.* Nashville: Broadman & Holman, 2003. This antigay marriage book accuses the gay rights movement of seeking to unfairly dominate other American interest groups.

Peter Sprigg, *Outrage: How Gay Activists and Liberal Judges Are Trashing Democracy to Redefine Marriage.* Washington, DC: Regnery, 2004. Argues that traditional marriage needs to be defended from renegade judiciaries.

Glenn T. Stanton and Bill Maier, *Marriage on Trial: The Case Against Same-Sex Marriage and Parenting.* Downers Grove, IL: InterVarsity Press, 2004. Defends a narrow definition of marriage in order to preserve society.

Andrew Sullivan, *Same-Sex Marriage: Pro and Con: A Reader.* New York: Vintage Books, 2004. A useful collection of opinions both for and against gay marriage.

Greg Wharton and Ian Philips, *I Do/I Don't: Queers on Marriage.* San Francisco: Suspect Thoughts Press, 2004. Explores the diverse and often contradictory opinions on gay marriage held by American homosexuals.

Evan Wolfson, *Why Marriage Matters: America, Equality, and Gay People's Right to Marry.* New York: Simon & Schuster, 2004. The author argues that marriage is a civil right that should be extended to gay couples.

Periodicals

Against the Current, "Gay Marriage, Yes!" May/June 2004.

Robert Benne and Gerald McDermott, "Gay Unions Undermine Society," *Roanoke Times,* February 22, 2004.

Christopher S. Bentley, "The Assault on Marriage," *New American,* April 19, 2004.

Mark David Blum, "A Matter of Personal Freedom: What's Love Got to Do with State-Sanctioned Marriage?" *(Syracuse, NY) Post-Standard,* December 2, 2004.

Patrick J. Buchanan, "Time for a New Boston Tea Party," *Wanderer,* December 4, 2003.

Charles Colson, "Societal Suicide: Legalizing Gay Marriage Will Lead to More Family Breakdown and Crime," *Christianity Today,* June 2004.

George Detweiler, "How to Protect Marriage," *New American,* August 9, 2004.

James Driscoll, "New Gay Political Strategies: Better Results Call for Better Leadership," *Washington Times,* November 18, 2004.

Kevin Duchschere, "Is Gay Marriage a Civil-Rights Issue? Five Black Leaders Say It's Not the Same," *(Minneapolis) Star Tribune,* March 26, 2004.

Lisa Duggan, "Holy Matrimony," *Nation,* March 15, 2004.

Economist, "The Case for Gay Marriage," February 28, 2004.

Richard A. Epstein, "Live and Let Live," *Wall Street Journal,* July 13, 2004.

(Eugene, OR) Register-Guard, "Leave Constitution Alone," February 25, 2004.

Sadie Fields, "The Gay Marriage Amendment: Can't Let the Few Hurt Society as a Whole," *Atlanta Journal-Constitution,* October 25, 2004.

Nathaniel Frank, "Perverted—Quack Gay Marriage Science," *New Republic,* May 3, 2004.

Robert P. George and David L. Tubbs, "Redefining Marriage Away," *City Journal,* Summer 2004.

E.J. Graff, "Are We Hitched Yet?" *Out,* October 2002.

Paul Greenberg, "Gay Marriage and Its Discontents," *Conservative Chronicle,* April 7, 2004.

Kim Grossnicklaus, "Gay Marriages Deprive the Children," *(Eugene, OR) Register-Guard,* March 8, 2004.

Hank Kalet, "Tying the Knot: First Step in Massachusetts," *Progressive Populist,* June 15, 2004.

Thomas M. Keane Jr., "Not Every Church Fears Gay Marriage," *Boston Herald,* February 11, 2004.

Douglas R. Kmiec, "Family Matters," *Los Angeles Times,* March 14, 2004.

Stanley Kurtz, "Beyond Gay Marriage," *Weekly Standard,* August 4–11, 2003.

David Limbaugh, "'Gay Marriage' Is Not About 'Rights,'" Townhall.com, February 27, 2004.

Los Angeles Times, "The Meaning of Marriage," July 16, 2004.

Howard Manly, "Gay vs. Civil Rights Fight Misses Point," *Boston Herald,* March 9, 2004.

Karla Mantilla, "Gay Marriage: Destroying the Family to Save the Children?" *Off Our Backs,* May/June 2004.

Edwin Meese, "A Shotgun Amendment," *Wall Street Journal,* March 10, 2004.

Mark Morford, "Where Is My Gay Apocalypse?" SFGate.com, March 5, 2004.

Tiffany L. Palmer, "Family Matters: Establishing Legal Parental Rights for Same-Sex Parents and Their Children," *Human Rights,* Summer 2003.

Ramesh Ponnuru, "Coming Out Ahead: Why Gay Marriage Is on the Way," *National Review,* July 28, 2003.

Deb Price, "Sullying the Constitution an Affront to All," *Liberal Opinion Week,* March 15, 2004.

Jonathan Rauch, "Power of Two," *New York Times Magazine,* March 7, 2004.

Revolutionary Worker, "The Insane Ravings of the Marriage Police," August 17, 2003.

Jim Rinnert, "The Trouble with Gay Marriage," *In These Times,* January 19, 2004.

Rocky Mountain News, "Who Decides Gay Marriage?" March 7, 2004.

Rosemary Radford Ruether, "Diverse Forms of Family Life Merit Recognition," *National Catholic Reporter,* June 16, 2000.

William Rusher, "Let the States Decide What 'Marriage' Is," WorldNetDaily.com, March 4, 2004.

Amelia Saletan, "Less Sanctimony, More Matrimony," Benladner.com, January 25, 2004.

Rick Santorum, "Defend Marriage Now," *Crisis Magazine,* September 1, 2003.

Shelby Steele, "Selma to San Francisco?" *Wall Street Journal,* March 18, 2004.

Mark Steyn, "Marital Strife," *National Review,* December 22, 2003.

Lynne Stoecklein, "Love Is Blind," *Denver Post,* April 11, 2004.

Trevor Thomas, "Someday, I Want to Get Married: Gay Marriage Should Be Debated in Human Terms," *Grand Rapids Press,* July 25, 2004.

Thomas Tryon, "Conservative Arguments Compel Support for Gay Marriage," *Sarasota Herald Tribune,* March 14, 2004.

Norah Vincent, "Gays Won't Tear Marriage Asunder," *Los Angeles Times,* July 17, 2003.

Web Sites

Alliance for Marriage (www.allianceformarriage.org/site/PageServer). A nonprofit organization devoted to traditional family values, this antigay marriage Web site includes news updates, articles, and speeches. Also available is information on the proposed Federal Marriage Amendment, which was written and heavily lobbied for by Alliance for Marriage.

American Family Association (www.afa.net). This group is concerned with preserving traditional family values and rejecting gay marriage, abortion, pornography, and gambling. A section on Special Projects details their ongoing boycotts of companies they believe threaten family values.

Don'tAmend.com (www.dontamend.com). Don'tAmend.com is a Web campaign that was launched in 2003 to prevent the Constitution from being amended to specify marriage as an institution between a man and a woman. Contains up-to-date information on protest events and rallies to halt the proposed amendment.

Equal Marriage for Same-Sex Couples (www.samesexmarriage.ca). This exhaustive pro-gay marriage Web site is based in Canada, where some provinces have legalized same-sex marriages. Includes news updates, articles, history, legal briefs, and more.

Human Rights Campaign (www.hrc.org). Human Rights Campaign, America's largest gay and lesbian organization, works to secure rights for gays, lesbians, bisexuals, and transgendered individuals. The Web site includes a section on issues surrounding gay marriage.

INDEX

PICTURE CREDITS

ABOUT THE EDITOR

Lauri S. Friedman earned her bachelor's degree in religion and political science from Vassar College. Much of her studies there focused on political Islam, and she produced a thesis on the Islamic revolution in Iran titled *Neither West, Nor East, but Islam*. She also holds a preparatory degree in flute performance from the Manhattan School of Music, and is pursuing a master's degree in history at San Diego State University. She has edited over ten books for Greenhaven Press, including *At Issue: What Motivates Suicide Bombers?*, *At Issue: How Should the United States Treat Prisoners in the War on Terror?*, and *Introducing Issues with Opposing Viewpoints: Terrorism.* She currently lives near the beach in San Diego with her yellow lab, Trucker.